Ten-Minute Math

Mathematics Activities and Games For Grades 3–5

Cornelia Tierney and Susan Jo Russell

Contributions by
Michael T. Battista
Mary Berle-Carmen
Douglas H. Clements
Karen Economopoulos
Marlene Kliman
Jan Mokros
Ricardo Nemirovsky
Andee Rubin

Administration and Production
Juania Ashley
Megan Murray

Dale Seymour Publications®

The preparation of this work was supported by National Science Foundation Grant ESI-9050210. However, any opinions or recommendations expressed herein are those of the authors and do not necessarily reflect the views of the National Science Foundation.

This project was supported, in part, by the

National Science Foundation

Opinions expressed are those of the authors and not necessarily those of the Foundation

Project Editor: Beverly Cory
Production/Manufacturing Director: Janet Yearian
Senior Production/Manufacturing Coordinator: Roxanne Knoll
Design Director: Jim O'Shea
Cover Design: Elaine Lopez
Text Design: Monika Popowitz
Illustrations: Carl Yoshihara © Pearson Learning.

The activities and games in *Ten-Minute Math* were previously published in a different form in the K–5 *Investigations in Number, Data, and Space*® curriculum (Dale Seymour Publications, 1998).

Dale Seymour Publications
299 Jefferson Road
Parsippany, New Jersey 07054

Order number DS21260
ISBN 0-86651-847-9

Contents

Introduction

Ten-Minute Math

The activities and games in this *Ten-Minute Math* book originated as part of the K–5 mathematics curriculum, *Investigations in Number, Data, and Space®*. In that program, the suggestions for quick explorations known as "ten-minute math" are woven throughout grades 3 through 5 to support and balance the in-depth work of each unit. In addition, the curriculum includes several math games that can be repeated often for skill-building work. Many *Investigations* teachers have asked that the Ten-Minute Math activities and the games that are embedded in *Investigations* be assembled in a single, easy-to-access collection. That collection is what you now hold in your hands.

Whether or not you use the *Investigations* units in your classroom, this book is a valuable resource for ongoing work in three major areas of the elementary mathematics curriculum: number, data analysis, and two- and three-dimensional space (geometry). With the activities in these three areas, you can help your students acquire broader mathematical thinking and problem-solving skills. You will also help them increase their repertoire of strategies for mental calculation, gain confidence in inventing their own approaches for solving problems, and become more fluent in reflecting on and articulating their problem-solving processes as they compare their techniques with those of their classmates.

Although you see just 21 activities and games listed in the contents, this collection in fact offers hundreds of ideas. Each activity is a template that can be adapted and varied for repeated use throughout grades 3–5. All the offerings in this book can be readily adapted to suit the needs of a particular class, and some can be varied to address different topics. For nearly any activity, you have many choices, allowing you to tailor the work to your particular situation. For example, you can decide

- how students are to work—as a whole class? in small groups? in pairs? individually?

- what tools students may to use to find their solutions—manipulatives such as interlocking cubes or pattern blocks? calculators? paper and pencil?

- how students are to share and reflect on their solutions and their strategies for arriving at them—with partners? in writing? as part of a whole-class discussion?

You can also easily adjust the particular content or the level of difficulty for these activities and games. For example, consider the activity *Guess My Number*. One teacher might choose clues that lead students to focus on number characteristics:

> Guess my number. It has two digits. It is less than 50. One of its digits is 3 more than the other. The sum of the digits is 11.

Another teacher may use the same format to focus on factor and multiple relationships:

> Guess my number. It is a multiple of 9. It is a factor of 72. It has two digits. It is a square number.

But the same activity can also work for fractions:

> Guess my number. It is between one-half and one. Its numerator is 3. It is a multiple of one-fourth.

In this way, the basic activity can be endlessly varied and extended, yet within a familiar format that students will recognize from one year to the next. Other activities even offer variations across content areas; for example, the geometry activity *Quick Images* has a variation that relates to number, and the data activity *Guess My Rule* has variations suitable for work with both number and two-dimensional geometric shapes.

What's the best way to use these Ten-Minute Math activities and games? You might distribute them throughout the school year in a variety of ways. As part of the *Investigations* curriculum, Ten-Minute Math is suggested not to reiterate but to complement the content of particular units. Thus, activities in geometry and data are often found in number units, whereas those focusing on number often appear in the data and geometry units. Through this dovetailed approach, students get continued exposure to and practice with each content area throughout the year. A chart showing the *Investigations* units in which each activity or game appears is included at the end of this collection.

If you are using only some of the *Investigations* units or are using a different curriculum, you may similarly choose particular activities and games in counterpoint to a particular content focus. Alternatively, you might choose activities to give depth or provide additional experiences within the same content area, or simply to help students develop broader skills in mathematical thinking and problem solving.

Because Ten-Minute Math activities are relatively short, they can be done at any time during the school day. As part of the *Investigations* curriculum, they are to be done *outside* of math time as a way to offer mathematical experiences throughout the day. Some teachers use them to bring the whole class together just before or after lunch, gym, or recess, or at the beginning or end of the day. Other teachers make the needed materials available to students throughout the day, to be used whenever they have free time or at teacher-specified times, such as indoor recess. Still others ask students to take home these activities and games to do with family members.

Ten-Minute Math experiences, games, and problems have proved so robust and easy to present in different versions that teachers find students eager to do them again and again, all year long, from one grade to the next.

Activities and Games at a Glance

Ten-Minute Math

Activities for Number

Calendar Math

(page 8) Students write a numerical expression that is equal to "today's" date. For example, if the date is March 19, students look for ways to combine numbers and operations to make 19. From day to day, teachers may introduce constraints on what numbers or operations students can use.

Counting Around the Class

(page 12) Students skip count around the class by a given number, such as twos, fives, or nines. As students become adept, they figure out how many of their classmates have already counted when a certain number is reached; they then predict the final number.

Seeing Numbers

(page 16) Arranging small objects in certain patterns or in groups can make it easy to see how many objects there are. For example, 3 rows of 4 squares is easily recognized as 12. When the teacher presents such an arrangement, students describe the number relationships that help them "see" the number and then rearrange the objects to represent different number relationships.

Guess My Number

(page 21) The teacher or leader chooses a secret number and gives initial hints about its characteristics (e.g., smaller than 50, multiple of 3, two digits). Students ask questions to narrow the possibilities until they deduce the secret number. Variations include Guess My Unit (focusing on measurement terminology) and Number Puzzles.

Estimation and Number Sense

(page 31) The teacher displays an arithmetic problem for about a minute while students try to mentally estimate the answer. After discussing their estimates and the strategies they used, students mentally find the precise solution.

Broken Calculator

(page 35) The teacher establishes a number that students must get on their calculator displays while pretending that certain keys are broken. The broken keys, which cannot be used, might be operations, numbers, or both. For example, students might be challenged to make 1,000 with the zero key "broken." After students find one solution, they find a series of related solutions by making small changes in the original one.

Nearest Answer

(page 39)   Students estimate answers to computation problems that they see only briefly and pick the closest answer from several that are given. This activity provides practice with approximating and with mental computation, a kind of thinking that helps in checking answers found by calculator.

Activities for Data and Probability

Likely or Unlikely?

(page 50)   Students propose real-world events, such as "School will be canceled next Tuesday because of a snowstorm," and judge the likelihood of these events. Initially they group their proposed events into two categories, Likely and Unlikely, then gradually increase the number of categories (for example, Very Likely, More Likely, Less Likely, and Very Unlikely) to make finer distinctions about the probability of various events.

Exploring Data

(page 53)   The class chooses a question to investigate about themselves, such as "How many different states have you visited?" The teacher quickly represents the data in a line plot, list, table, or bar graph. Students discuss what they can tell from the data, what new questions this information leads to, and what predictions they can make.

What Is Likely?

(page 56)   Given a transparent container with objects of two different colors, students predict the likelihood of randomly picking certain colors or combinations of colors. They pick out ten objects, record the colors, and compare the outcome with their predictions. This exploration of sampling also develops concrete meaning for ratio and proportion.

Guess My Rule

(page 59)   In this classification game, a teacher or leader secretly establishes a "rule" that describes certain items and then gives examples of items that do and do not fit the rule. Students use this evidence to form hypotheses, then systematically suggest other items in order to deduce the rule. Variations include guessing the shared attributes of people, numbers, and two-dimensional shapes.

Graph Stories

(page 67)   Students look at an unlabeled graph and, from its distinctive shape, try to imagine what story this graph could be telling. In addition, they draw graphs to fit given stories. This helps students move beyond the particular numbers on a graph to focus on and interpret important qualities of the whole shape.

Activities for Geometry and Shape

Quick Images

(page 74)   The teacher briefly shows a geometric design and then covers it. Students recreate the design from their mental image of it by making a drawing (for 2-D designs) or putting together interlocking cubes (for 3-D designs). This helps students focus on spatial relationships and patterns in 2-D and 3-D figures. A variation with dot patterns is similar to the Seeing Numbers activity.

Length and Perimeter

(page 85)   This is an off-computer activity for students who are using the computer program Geo-Logo, in particular the "repeat" command. Students plan several ways to use repeat commands to send the Geo-Logo turtle a certain distance or to draw a regular polygon. They also predict the distance or the shape that will result from certain commands.

Volume and Surface Area

(page 89)   When presented with an image of a solid constructed from cubes, students figure out its volume (or number of cubes used to make it) and its surface area (or number of square "stamps" needed to cover the outside of the solid). In a variation, they discover that 3-D objects with the same volume do not necessarily have the same surface area.

Number Games

Close to 100

(page 96)   Players use randomly drawn digits to make pairs of numbers that, when added, total as close as possible to 100. This game develops understanding of place value and the relative size of numbers. Players also work out strategies for estimating, adding two-digit numbers, and subtracting numbers from 100. Variations include Close to 1,000 (making number pairs that total or nearly total 1,000) and Close to 0 (making number pairs with a difference as close as possible to 0).

Capture 5

(page 105) Together players set up the Capture 5 gameboard (a 100 chart) by placing a game piece for each player and 12 markers on random numbers. Players are then dealt cards for positive and negative multiples of 1 and 10 (including +1, −1, +2, −2, +3, −3, +10, −10, +20, −20, +30, −30). By combining their cards with numbers on the board, players move to "capture" the marker in a particular square. For example, a player starting on 35 might use the cards +20 and −2 to reach the square for 53. The goal is to capture five markers.

Fraction Cookie Game

(page 110) Players roll a fraction die or draw a fraction card to determine what fraction of a "cookie" (hexagonal pattern block) they may add to their collection. Variations include subtracting pieces from whole cookies and doing a mix of adding and subtracting. The object is to be the first to collect or give away a particular number of whole hexagon cookies.

Digits Game

(page 114) Players choose a target number, such as 1,000, and rearrange randomly drawn digits to make numbers as close as possible to that target. For example, given the digits 2, 3, 5, 7, and 8, the closest number to 1,000 would be 875. This game builds understanding of place value and the role of zero in a place value system, as well as strategies for comparing numbers.

Estimation Game

(page 118) The game leader presents a problem template (such as __ __ __ × __ __), deals a number card to fill each slot, and then reveals the problem. Players must quickly estimate the answer. At the end of each round, players determine their scores by finding the difference between their estimate and the actual answer.

Multiple Bingo and Division Bingo

(page 122) In these two versions of the classic game, the "Bingo" grid is either a 100 chart (for Multiple Bingo) or a multiplication table (for Division Bingo). Players select number cards from special decks and find either a multiple or a factor of that number on their Bingo grid, then color in that square. The goal is to color in five consecutive numbers, horizontally, vertically, or diagonally.

Activities for Number

The activities in this section help students build a rich web of knowledge about numbers and operations. While students explore number relationships, number composition, and the structure of our number system, they are also developing meaning for the four basic operations and the relationships among them. Students have many opportunities to practice arithmetic as they devise their own strategies for computation and estimation, investigate equivalent numeric expressions, and share computational approaches with their peers.

For other ways of working with number, see the six games in the last section of this book, as well as variations to activities in the geometry and data sections.

In an activity sometimes called Today's Number, students write numerical expressions that are equal to the day's date. For example, if the date is March 19, students look for ways to combine numbers and operations to make 19. Constraints on the numbers or operations allowed encourage students to be flexible in their use of arithmetic skills. As students discuss principles or rules for "expressions that work," these quickly become a part of the mathematics culture in their class.

Materials

No special materials needed

Mathematical Emphasis

Calendar Math is a simple way of providing arithmetic practice and opportunities for students to share mathematical discoveries. The focus is on

- developing a web of numerical knowledge about any number
- using operations flexibly
- recognizing relationships among operations (for example, knowing that adding and then subtracting the same number has a net effect of 0)
- learning about and using key mathematical ideas, such as the effect of using an operation with 0 or 1
- deriving new numerical expressions by modifying a particular expression systematically (for example, if $2 + 9 = 11$, then so does $3 + 8$, $4 + 7$, $5 + 6$, and so forth)

Procedure

Step 1. Pose the problem. For example, "Today's date is September 12. Who can think of a way we could combine numbers to make 12?"

Step 2. List student responses. Their ideas might include expressions like these:

$$6 + 6$$
$$4 \times 3$$
$$12 + 0$$
$$\frac{1}{2} \times 24$$
$$3 - 3 + 6 + 6$$

Step 3. Choose a "favorite expression" for the day. Students choose their favorite from the listed expressions, perhaps the most unusual, or one that uses a new idea. Use the class favorite to write the date on the board:

September $(0 \times 12) + 12$.

Introducing Constraints

Introduce constraints based on your class's ease with particular operations and numbers. For example, if students are very comfortable with addition, eliminate addition as a possibility: "Today you can use any operation you want to use, *except* addition." You could also require that a certain operation or kind of number is used. Possible constraints include these:

You can't use any number that is a multiple of 2.

You can't use addition or subtraction.

You must use more than one operation.

You must use one number that is bigger than 100 (or 1,000 or 5,000).

You must start with 100.

You must use at least three numbers.

You can't use 0.

You must use at least one number that is smaller than 1.

You must use one negative number.

You can only use the digits 1, 2, 3, and 4.

Looking for Patterns

Encourage students to find expressions that they can alter systematically to find more expressions. For example, here is a pattern that a student devised for 20:

$$2 \times 10$$
$$2 \times 9 + 2$$
$$2 \times 8 + 4$$
$$2 \times 7 + 6$$
$$2 \times 6 + 8$$
$$2 \times 5 + 10$$

Developing Class "Rules"

Our experience is that, through this activity, new ideas about numbers become part of the culture of the classroom. For example, in one classroom, one student learned about square numbers and the notation for them. Because she used these numbers in Calendar Math, other students became familiar with them and were soon using numbers such as 4^2.

Other kinds of relationships are often discovered by one child and then become common knowledge. One day when a class was finding expressions equivalent to 14, a student suggested 14×0. This remark prompted a discussion of what happens when you multiply a number by 0, and students eventually concluded that the result of multiplying any number by 0 is 0. The teacher wrote this on a list of "rules" discovered over the course of the year. Following are some other rules students have discovered during this activity:

A number divided by 1 is the number.

A number multiplied by 1 is the number.

Any number multiplied by 0 is 0.

Any number divided by itself is 1.

Subtract or add 0 to any number and you still have the same number.

Adding lots of 0's doesn't change anything.

You can make any number by adding enough 1's to count up to that number.

Adding a number and then subtracting the same number is like adding 0.

Today's Date on the Calculator

Materials: Calculator for each student

For a quiet ten minutes, students work individually or in pairs to find ways to make the date, using their calculators. Make sure that they record their expressions on a piece of paper. They can choose their favorite solution and write it on the board. This is a good way for students to explore new keys on the calculator.

What Day of the Calendar Year Is It?

Challenge students to figure out what day of the (calendar) year it is. That is, "If there are 365 days in a year, and January 1 is day number 1, what number would today be?" You may want to generate a list of important information that students will need to solve this problem. For example, one class generated a chart that looked something like this:

28 or 29 days	30 days	31 days
February	September	January
	April	March
	June	May
	November	July
		August
		October
		December

365 days in a year

leap year every 4 years (366 days)

Is this year a leap year?

Once students are familiar with finding the number for any day of the year, ask them once in a while what fraction of the year that represents. "If today is day number 120, then we're $^{120}/_{365}$ of the way through the year. What familiar fraction is that closest to? About how far through the year are we? About how much do we have left to go?"

What Day of the School Year Is It?

Students could also figure out the number that tells what day of the school year "today" is. Remind them when the first day of school was. For example, "If September 7 was the first day of school this year, we can call it school day number 1. Then what number would today be?" Students will need to decide what to do about school holidays, vacations, and snow days. They can also figure out how many days are left in the school year, assuming no unexpected days off. Again, encourage students to determine what fraction of the school year has passed and what fraction is left.

Making More Expressions

Students could develop expressions that represent the month and the year. "Today's" date might then read something like this:

$$(3 \times 2) + 3 \qquad (0 \times 12) + 12 \qquad (1{,}000 \times 2) + 2$$

| September | 12 | 2002 |

Related Homework Option

Planning Ahead   Suggest that students think at home about how they might make the next day's date. Advise them of any constraints you have set, and ask them to figure out five different ways to make the date. They can share their favorite in class.

Students count around the class by a particular number, such as 2, 5, or 9. That is, if counting by 2, the first student says "2," the next student says "4," the next "6," and so forth. Before the count starts, students try to predict the ending number of the count, or the number the last person in class will say. During and after the count, students discuss relationships between the chosen factor and its multiples.

Materials

No special materials needed

Mathematical Emphasis

Counting Around the Class gives students practice with counting by many different numbers and fosters numerical reasoning about the relationships among factors and their multiples. The focus is on

- becoming familiar with multiplication patterns
- relating factors to their multiples
- developing number sense about multiplication and division relationships

Procedure

Step 1. Choose a number to count by. For example, if the class has been working with quarters recently, you might want to count by 25.

Step 2. Ask students to predict the target number. "If we count by 25 around the class, what number will the last person in the class say?" Encourage students to talk about how they could figure this out without doing the actual counting.

Step 3. Count around the class by your chosen number. "25 . . . 50 . . . 75 . . ." If some students seem uncertain about the number that comes next, you might write the numbers on the board as students say them. Seeing the visual patterns often helps students with the spoken pattern.

You might count around a second time by the same number, starting with a different person, so that students will hear the same pattern more than once and have their turns at different points in the sequence.

Step 4. Pause in the middle of the count to look back. "We're up to 375, counting by 25. How many students have we counted so far? How do you know?"

Step 5. Extend the problem. Ask questions like these:

"Which of your predictions were reasonable? Which were possible? Which were impossible?" (A student might remark, for example, "You couldn't have 510 for 25's because 25 only lands on the 25's, the 50's, the 75's, and the 100's.")

"What if we had 32 students in this class instead of 28? Then what would the ending number be?"

"What if we counted by a different number? This time we counted by 25 and ended on 700. What if we counted by 50? What do you think would be the ending number? Why do you think it will be twice as big? How did you figure that out?"

Special Notes

Let Students Prepare   Whenever you introduce an unfamiliar number to count by, students may need some preparation before they begin counting around the class. Ask students to work in pairs, with whatever materials they want, to determine the ending number for the count.

Avoid Competition   Be sensitive to potential embarrassment or competition that may occur if some students have difficulty figuring out their number. One teacher allowed students to volunteer for the next number, rather than counting in a particular order. Other teachers have made the count a cooperative effort, establishing an atmosphere in which students readily helped each other, and anyone felt free to ask for help.

Write the Numbers   Some students find patterns more easily by seeing the numbers than by hearing them. You might write the numbers on chart paper as they are said, or let students write them on their own paper.

Multiplication Practice

Count around the class by single-digit numbers to provide practice with multiplication (that is, count by 2, 3, 4, 5, 7, and so forth). When students first begin to count by numbers other than 1, they are usually most comfortable with 2, 5, and 10, which have very regular patterns. Soon they can begin to count by more difficult single-digit numbers: 3, 4, 6, and (later) 7, 8, and 9.

Landmark Numbers

While learning about money or about our base ten system of numeration, students can count by such "landmark" numbers as 20, 25, 50, 100, and 1,000. Fluency in moving among landmark numbers is especially valuable in mental computation. Counting by multiples of 10 and 100 (e.g., by 30, by 40, or by 600) will support students' growing familiarity with the base ten system of numeration.

Making Connections

When you choose harder numbers to count by, pick those that are related in some way to numbers students are very familiar with. For example, once students are comfortable counting by 25, have them count by 75. Ask students how knowing the 25's will help them count by 75. If students are fluent with 3's, try counting by 6 or by 30. If students are fluent with 5's, 10's and 20's, start working on 15. If they are comfortable counting by 15, ask them to count by 150 or 1,500.

Large Numbers

Introduce counting by large numbers, such as 2,000 or 5,000 or 1,500 or 10,000. Write the numbers or ask a student volunteer to write them as they are said.

What Could We Count By?

Specify a target number such as 100, or 50, or 1,000, or 24. Ask students to find a number they could count by so that someone in the class would say the number you have specified. Encourage them to share their strategies for figuring this out. Count around the class by the suggested numbers to see if they work.

Don't Start with 0

For some instances of counting around the class, start the count with a multiple other than 0. For example, students might count by 10 or 25, but you would set the starting number at 50, 100, 1,000, or 525.

Fractions and Decimals

As appropriate, count around the classroom by fractions or by decimal numbers. Begin with easier landmark numbers such as 0.5, 0.25, $\frac{1}{3}$, and $\frac{1}{4}$. Count by more difficult numbers (such as $\frac{3}{4}$, $1\frac{1}{2}$, 2.25, and 0.125) as you feel your students are ready. An interesting variation is to count by less-familiar decimals on the calculator (such as 0.21, 0.09, and 0.99) and discuss any patterns your students see.

Counting Backwards

Starting with a given number, count backwards around the class. Choose numbers with patterns that are already familiar to students. For example, start at 400 and count backwards by 2, 5, 10, or 25. As students become more comfortable with this variation, try counting by more difficult numbers. Or, play a modified version of What Could We Count By? Give students a starting number (such as 100 or 1,000) and ask them to find a number they could count by, backwards, that would land them exactly on 0 (or, so that someone will say a particular number during the count).

Skip Counting on the Calculator

Materials: Calculator for each student

On some days everyone or at least a few students might use calculators to skip count while you are counting around the class. On most calculators, the equals (=) key provides a built-in constant function, allowing you to skip count easily. For example, if you want to skip count by 25, you press your starting number (let's say 0), the operation you want to use (in this case, +), and the number you want to count by (in this case, 25). Then press the equals key each time you want to add 25. Thus, suppose you press the following sequence:

You will see on your screen 25, 50, 75, 100.

Related Homework Options

Counting Patterns   Students write out a counting pattern up to a target number (for example, counting by 25 up to 500). Then they write about the patterns they see in their counting. Calculators can be used for this.

Mystery Number Problems   Provide an ending number, and ask students to figure out a "mystery" factor they could count by to reach that target. For example: "I'm thinking of a mystery number. If we counted around the class by my mystery number today, we would get to 2,800. What could the mystery number be?"

Or, provide students with the final number and the factor. The problem is to figure out the number of students in the class. For example: "When a certain class counts by 25, the last student says 550. How many students are in that class?" Calculators can be used.

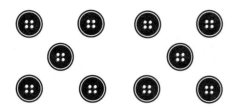

Students observe a particular number of objects arranged in such a way that the amount is easy to recognize on sight. Arrangements might include, for example, rectangular arrays or domino dot patterns. Students find different ways to describe number relationships that are apparent in the arrangement of objects. Then, they rearrange the objects to highlight other number relationships.

Materials

Overhead projector

Small objects such as counting chips, blocks, tiles, or buttons, 30–40 of one kind

Sheet of paper to cover the display

Two or three loops of string (to surround areas on the overhead projector), each about 12 inches in circumference

Mathematical Emphasis

Through the Seeing Numbers activity, students build their understanding of number and explore ways of representing these relationships. The focus is on

- exploring number relationships such as factors and fractions of a whole
- developing a visual model for factors, fractions, and partitions of a whole number
- finding different ways to represent number relationships, including fraction notation, factor pairs, and equations

Procedure

Preparation. Before turning on the overhead projector, arrange a composite number of small objects on the overhead in an array or other grouping that makes the number easy to recognize. Introduce the activity with a number that has only a few factors. For example, you might lay out the number 15 as a 3-by-5 array. You might arrange the number 25 as 5 clumps of 5 (in a domino dot pattern). Or you might arrange 24 objects in groups of 3, laid out in two rows of 4 groups each. (See the Sample Arrangements on page 18 for other ideas.)

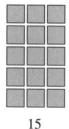

15

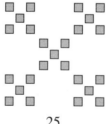

25

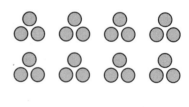

24

Step 1. Show the arrangement for 5 seconds. Then cover it.

Step 2. Students tell their neighbors what they saw. "How were the chips arranged? How many chips were there in all?" Students may want to draw their mental image of the arrangement to get a clearer picture of it.

Step 3. Display the arrangement again. This time leave the arrangement visible while students share how they see it. "How many chips are there? How did you figure out the number? Did anyone figure it out a different way?"

Step 4. Students write down some number relationships they see in the display. You might ask questions like these to get them started: "What smaller numbers can you see in this display of 24? What factor pairs do you see? In this arrangement, what numbers divide 24 evenly? What fractions of 24 can you see? Talk with your neighbors about what you notice. Explain what you see in the display that gives you these ideas."

Step 5. List student responses. As students describe the number relationships they see, write their statements as sentences and as equations. Confirm with individuals that you are correctly writing what they mean. Invite students to show how they are grouping the objects, or demonstrate it using a loop of string. For the suggested arrangement of 24, they might offer ideas like these:

Eight groups of three make twenty-four.

$8 \times 3 = 24$

Four times three plus four times three makes twenty-four. If you put one loop around the top line and the other around the bottom line, you have twelve in each. Twelve and twelve are twenty-four.

$(4 \times 3) + (4 \times 3) = 24$

Two times four times three is twenty-four. That's two rows, four groups in each row, three things in a group.

$2 \times 4 \times 3 = 24$

One-eighth of twenty-four is three. There are eight groups of three chips. You can see it in this way:

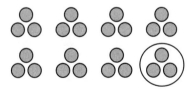

$\frac{1}{8}$ of $24 = 3$

Two-eighths of twenty-four is six. That's two groups of three.

$\frac{2}{8}$ of $24 = 6$

Step 6. Students suggest another arrangement of the same total. The new arrangement should show different number relationships. "How else might you arrange these objects to show different number relationships? to show different factors? What other fractions of 24 can we show?" For example, students might suggest a grouping that highlights the factors 6 and 4 and fractions that are sixths.

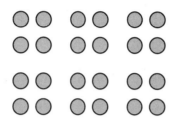

Sample Arrangements

Following are some other arrangements that highlight number relationships.

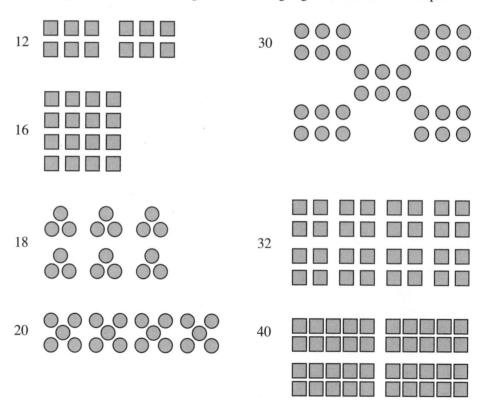

Large Numbers

Materials: Blank overhead transparencies

To explore large numbers, write numbers in special configurations on an overhead transparency instead of arranging objects. For example, you might write numbers in one of the following arrangements for 200:

20	20	20	20	20
20	20	20	20	20

4 x 10			4 x 10
	4 x 10		
4 x 10			4 x 10

Generating Number Sentences

Given an arrangement of either objects or numbers (as in the Large Number variation), you can focus the activity on writing equations and other notations for computation. Working alone or in pairs, students generate as many number statements as they can about the arrangement you are showing. Pool all the different statements, perhaps by asking pairs of students to each write one of their equations on the board. Here are some possibilities for an arrangement of 24 chips in 3 groups of 8:

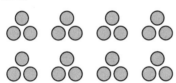

$\frac{24}{8} = 3$ $\frac{1}{8}$ of 24 = 3

$\frac{2}{8}$ of 24 = 6 $\frac{1}{4} \times 24 = 6$

$\frac{3}{4} \times 12 = 9$ $24 \div 3 = 8$

$3 \times 8 = 24$ $12 + 12 = 24$

$3 + 3 + 3 + 3 = 12$

$$\begin{array}{r} 4 \\ \times\, 3 \\ \hline 12 \end{array}$$

$8\overline{)24}^{\,3}$

Fractions of Different Shapes and Colors

Materials: Small objects of many different shapes, and transparent colored shapes

Put a mixture of 5–10 small objects on the overhead. You might use a combination of paper clips, erasers, pattern blocks, counting chips, magnetic letters or numbers, and plastic objects in familiar shapes (animals, trees, houses, people, boats, cars, and so forth). Include transparent shapes in colors if you have some. Students make statements that tell about parts of the whole. Start with "___ out of ___" statements, and later ask for fraction statements. For example:

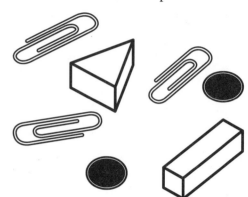

3 out of 7 are paper clips.

2 out of 7 are round.

$\frac{3}{7}$ of the objects are paper clips.

$\frac{2}{7}$ of the objects are round.

Related Homework Option

"Show and Tell" Numbers   Assign a particular number for homework. "How could you show this number? What can you tell us about this number?" Students draw one or more arrangements of objects and make a list of statements that describe number relationships related to each arrangement.

Guess My Number

You choose a mystery number and give clues about the characteristics of the number. For example: "It is less than 50. It is a multiple of 7. One of its digits is two more than the other digit." Students work in pairs to identify the mystery number. If more than one solution fits the clues, they may ask yes-or-no questions to narrow the field. They might ask, for example, "Is the number less than 40? Is the number a multiple of 5?"

Mathematical Emphasis

Guess My Number involves students in logical reasoning as they apply your _____ to eliminate those that do not fit. Students _____ eory as they learn to recognize and describe _____ lationships among numbers. The focus is on

- _____ lities
- _____ s
- _____ eliminate possible solutions
- _____ numbers, such as which are multiples or
- _____ ns that describe numbers
- _____ uess My Unit variation)

_____ u may want to write it down so that you

_____ es, you might choose clues so that only _____ es, you might choose clues so that several _____ that describe number characteristics and rela- _____ es, the number of digits, and odd and even.

_____ **to find numbers that fit the clues.** Provide a 100 chart (or 300 chart) and scraps of paper or numeral cards for students to use to record numbers they think might fit the clues. Give students just one or two minutes to find numbers they think might work.

Step 4. Record all suggested solutions. To get responses from every student, you may want to ask students to record their solutions on scraps of paper and hold them up on a given signal. Some teachers provide numeral cards that students can hold up to show their solution (for example, they might hold up a 2 and a 1 together to show 21). List on the board all solutions that students propose. Everyone looks

Materials
100 chart (p. 26) for each student

300 chart, for a larger range of numbers (p. 27)

Scraps of paper or numeral cards (optional, for showing solutions)

over all the proposed solutions and challenge any that they think don't fit all the clues. Challengers must give the reasons for their challenges.

Step 5. Invite students to ask further questions. If more than one solution fits all the clues, students must ask yes-or-no questions to try to eliminate some of the possibilities, until only one solution remains. You can erase numbers as students' questions eliminate them (be sure to let students tell you which numbers to erase). Encourage students to ask questions that might eliminate more than one of the proposed solutions.

New Number Characteristics

During the year, vary this game to include mathematical terms that have come up in your mathematics class. For example, clues might speak of square numbers, prime numbers, odd and even numbers, factors, multiples, doubling (tripling, halving), *less than* and *more than* concepts, as well as the number of digits involved.

Large Numbers

Begin with numbers under 100, but gradually expand the range of numbers that you include in your clues to larger numbers with which your students have been working. For example:

> It is a multiple of 50.
> It has three digits.
> Two of its digits are the same.
> It is not a multiple of 100.

Don't Share Solutions Until the End

As students become more practiced in formulating questions to eliminate possible solutions, you may want to skip step 4, "Record all suggested solutions." That is, while student pairs still find all solutions they think are possible, these are not shared and posted in class. Rather, students ask yes-or-no questions in a whole-class discussion, but privately eliminate numbers on their own list of solutions. When students have no more questions, they volunteer their solutions and explain why they think their answer is correct.

Guess My Fraction

Pick a fraction. Tell students whether it is smaller than $1/2$, between $1/2$ and 1, between 1 and 2, or bound by any other familiar numbers. You might use additional clues like these:

It is a multiple of $1/4$ (for example, $1/2$, $3/4$, 1, or $1^1/4$).

The numerator is 2 (for example, $2/3$ or $2/5$).

You can make it with pattern blocks (for example, $2/3$ or $5/6$).

Number Puzzles

Materials: Puzzles with four clues, similar to Miranda's Number Puzzle (p. 28)

Write your own number puzzles with exactly four clues. Miranda's Number Puzzle is one example; some others are listed below. You may create puzzles with only one solution, with several correct answers, or with no possible solution at all. Writing your own puzzle clues enables you to adjust the level of difficulty to a particular class or group.

Write each clue on a separate strip and store them in prepared envelopes (one envelope for each set of clues) for the class to share. Clearly identify each puzzle envelope with a number, letter, or name (e.g., Andre's puzzle) so that students can keep track of which ones they have solved. Working in groups of four, students choose a puzzle and each take one clue. They read the clues to one another and work together to narrow down the possible solutions. Set up a pool where groups can trade in their envelopes as they finish with each puzzle.

The *Investigations* unit *Introduction to Mathematical Thinking at Grade 5* includes many puzzles of this type. Students who have done that unit will have experience working in groups to solve them. The following examples show a range of problem types to get you started.

Andre's number is a square number.
Andre's number is a cube.
Andre's number is even.
Andre's number is smaller than 100.

Brigitta's number is a factor of 36.
Brigitta's number is a multiple of 3.
Brigitta's number is even.
Brigitta's number is a multiple of 9.

One-third of Cezar's number is a prime number.
One more than Cezar's number is a square number.
Twice Cezar's number is a multiple of 10.
Cezar's number is a factor of 60.

Danisha's number is a multiple of 6.
Danisha's number is a multiple of 14.
Danisha's number is not a multiple of 4.
The sum of its digits is 6.

Eric's number is a factor of 72.
Eric's number is larger than 6.
Eric's number is a square number.
Eric's number has one digit.

Fiona's number is even.
Fiona's number is not a multiple of 4.
Fiona's number is between 30 and 40.
The sum of its digits is 11.

Greg's number is a multiple of 15.
Greg's number is between 200 and 300.
Greg's number is a multiple of 7.
Greg's number is an even number.

Holly's number is a multiple of 25.
Holly's number is not a multiple of 50.
Holly's number is between 200 and 300.
Holly's number has three different digits.

Isaac's number is a square number.
Isaac's number is odd.
Isaac's number is larger than 150.
Isaac's number is smaller than 200.

Jamilla's number is double a prime number.
Jamilla's number is 3 times a prime number.
Jamilla's number is one digit.
Jamilla's number is even.

Kyle's number is a multiple of 25.
Kyle's number is a factor of 300.
Kyle's number has three digits.
Two digits in Kyle's number are the same.

Laurel's number is a multiple of 12.
Laurel's number is a multiple of 150.
Laurel's number is a multiple of 40.
Laurel's number is smaller than 700.

Guess My Unit

Materials: Deck of Guess My Unit cards (pp. 29–30) for each pair or small group

This variation, in which students guess a unit of measurement instead of a number, appears in the *Investigations* fifth grade *Measurement Benchmarks* unit. Each pair or group of students should have a complete set of Guess My Unit cards, displayed face up on their desks. Pick a measurement unit from those on the cards, or choose one of your own. If you create a new unit card, make sure each deck has that card.

Follow the same procedure as for Guess My Number. Give students a few beginning clues that focus on the characteristics and relationships among measurement units. For example:

> It is a measurement of weight.
> It is a metric unit.
> It is equal to a little over two pounds.

As you state the initial clues, record them where students can refer to them. Give students a few minutes to work together to discover your unit. They might flip over or set aside any cards that your clues have eliminated as possibilities. If they do not yet have enough information, they ask yes-or-no questions until they can identify the mystery unit.

Calculator Guess My Number

Materials: Calculator for each student

Present clues that provide opportunities for computation using a calculator. For example:

> It is larger than 35×20.
> It is smaller than $1,800 \div 2$.
> One of its factors is 25.
> None of its digits is 7.

Related Homework Options

Guess My Number Homework   Prepare a sheet with one or two Guess My Number problems for students to work on at home. As part of their work, students should write whether they think only one number fits the clues or whether several numbers fit. If only one solution exists, how do they know it is the only number that fits the clues? If more than one solution is possible, do they think they have them all? How do they know?

Students' Mystery Choices   Each student chooses a number or measurement unit and develops clues to present to the rest of the class. You'll probably want to have students submit their clues and solutions to you for advance review. If the clues are too broad (if, for example, 50 solutions are possible) or if they unintentionally yield no solution, ask the students to revise their clues. Once you approve the clues, students are in charge of presenting them, running the discussion, and answering all questions about their mystery choice during a Ten-Minute Math session.

Students might also create their own four-clue number puzzles and exchange them with other groups during a Ten-Minute Math session. Be sure to review the puzzles before they are shared. If necessary, remind groups that puzzles may have one solution, more than one solution, or possibly no solution at all.

Guess My Number

1	2	3	4	5	6	7	8	9	10
11	12	13	14	15	16	17	18	19	20
21	22	23	24	25	26	27	28	29	30
31	32	33	34	35	36	37	38	39	40
41	42	43	44	45	46	47	48	49	50
51	52	53	54	55	56	57	58	59	60
61	62	63	64	65	66	67	68	69	70
71	72	73	74	75	76	77	78	79	80
81	82	83	84	85	86	87	88	89	90
91	92	93	94	95	96	97	98	99	100

300 Chart

1	2	3	4	5	6	7	8	9	10
11	12	13	14	15	16	17	18	19	20
21	22	23	24	25	26	27	28	29	30
31	32	33	34	35	36	37	38	39	40
41	42	43	44	45	46	47	48	49	50
51	52	53	54	55	56	57	58	59	60
61	62	63	64	65	66	67	68	69	70
71	72	73	74	75	76	77	78	79	80
81	82	83	84	85	86	87	88	89	90
91	92	93	94	95	96	97	98	99	100
101	102	103	104	105	106	107	108	109	110
111	112	113	114	115	116	117	118	119	120
121	122	123	124	125	126	127	128	129	130
131	132	133	134	135	136	137	138	139	140
141	142	143	144	145	146	147	148	149	150
151	152	153	154	155	156	157	158	159	160
161	162	163	164	165	166	167	168	169	170
171	172	173	174	175	176	177	178	179	180
181	182	183	184	185	186	187	188	189	190
191	192	193	194	195	196	197	198	199	200
201	202	203	204	205	206	207	208	209	210
211	212	213	214	215	216	217	218	219	220
221	222	223	224	225	226	227	228	229	230
231	232	233	234	235	236	237	238	239	240
241	242	243	244	245	246	247	248	249	250
251	252	253	254	255	256	257	258	259	260
261	262	263	264	265	266	267	268	269	270
271	272	273	274	275	276	277	278	279	280
281	282	283	284	285	286	287	288	289	290
291	292	293	294	295	296	297	298	299	300

✂ ---

Miranda's number is greater than 50.

✂ ---

Miranda's number is less than 100.

✂ ---

Miranda's number is a multiple of 12.

✂ ---

Miranda's number is a multiple of 14.

✂ ---

Guess My Number

mile	yard	foot
inch	kilometer	meter
centimeter	millimeter	

ton	pound	ounce
kilogram	gram	milligram

gallon	quart	pint
cup	tablespoon	teaspoon
liter	milliliter	cubic centimeter

second	minute	hour
day	week	month
year	decade	century

Estimation and Number Sense

Students mentally estimate the answer to an arithmetic problem that they see displayed for a brief time. They discuss their estimates and their strategies. Then they find a precise solution to the problem by using mental computation strategies.

$$8 \times 57 \approx$$

Mathematical Emphasis

Through Estimation and Number Sense, students develop strategies for mental computation and for judging the reasonableness of the results of a computation done on paper or with a calculator. The focus is on

- looking at a problem as a whole
- breaking apart, reordering, or combining numbers within a problem for easier computation
- looking at the largest part of each number first (looking at hundreds before tens, thousands before hundreds, and so forth)

Materials
No special materials needed

Procedure

Step 1. Present a problem. Write a computation problem on the chalkboard or overhead. For example:

$$9 + 25 + 11$$

Step 2. Allow less than a minute to think about the problem. In the allotted time, students come up with the best estimate they can. This estimate might be, but will not usually be, an exact answer. Students do not write anything down or use the calculator during this time.

Step 3. Cover the problem and ask students to discuss what they know. "What did you notice about the numbers in this problem? Did you estimate an answer? How did you make your estimate?"

Encourage all kinds of estimation statements and strategies. Some will be more general; others may be quite precise:

> "It's at least 35 because I saw 25 and a number in the tens."

> "I think it's less than 100 because 25 was the biggest number and there were only three numbers."

> "I think it's 25 + 20 because I saw the 9 + 11 and that's 20, and then add on 25 and that gets you to 45."

Be sure that you continue to encourage a variety of observations, especially the "more than, less than" statements, even if some students have solved it exactly.

Step 4. Uncover the problem and continue the discussion. "What do you notice now? What do you think about your estimates? Do you want to change them? What are some mental strategies you can use to solve the problem exactly?"

Problems That Can Be Reordered

Give problems like the following examples, in which regrouping the numbers in particular ways can help students find the answer easily.

$$6 + 2 - 4 + 1 - 5 + 4 + 5 - 2$$

$$36 + 22 + 4 + 8$$

$$112 - 30 + 60 - 2$$

$$654 - 12 + 300 + 112$$

$$65 - 48 + 5 - 2$$

$$15 + 75 + 210 + 10$$

$$3 \times 14 \div 7$$

Encourage students to look at each problem as a whole before they start. Rather than taking each number and operation in sequence, they look first to see what numbers are easy to put together to get answers to part of the problem. Then they combine their partial results to answer the whole problem.

Large Numbers

Present problems that require students to "think from left to right" and to round numbers to "nice numbers" in order to come up with a good estimate. For example:

$$130 + 243 + 492$$

$$10,981 + 5,003 + 99,000$$

$$3,891 - 403$$

$$2,769 \div 2$$

$$\begin{array}{r} 723 \\ 481 \\ + 198 \\ \hline \end{array}$$

$$\begin{array}{r} 697 \\ \times \ 3 \\ \hline \end{array}$$

Present problems in both horizontal and vertical formats. If the vertical format triggers a rote procedure of starting from the right and "carrying," encourage students to look at the numbers as a whole and to think about the largest parts of the numbers first. Thus, for the problem $130 + 243 + 492$, they might think first, "492 is about 500." Then, thinking in terms of the largest part of the numbers first (hundreds), they might reason: "200 and 500 is 700, and 100 more is 800, and then there's some extra, so I think it's a little over 800."

Fractions

Pose problems with fractions and ask students to estimate the number of wholes the result is closest to. Start with problems such as these:

$$\frac{1}{2} + \frac{1}{3} \qquad \frac{1}{2} + \frac{3}{4}$$

Ask, "Is the answer more than or less than 1?" Then you can include less familiar fractions in problems such as the following, expanding the question to "Is the answer closer to 0, 1, or 2?"

$$\frac{5}{8} + \frac{5}{9} \qquad \frac{1}{11} + \frac{2}{9} + \frac{1}{15}$$

Begin to include problems that multiply fractions by whole numbers:

$$5 \times \frac{1}{4} \qquad 3 \times \frac{1}{8}$$

Eventually, use fractions with numerators larger than the denominators and ask, "About how many wholes are in this fraction?" For example:

$$\frac{9}{4} \qquad \frac{50}{7} \qquad \frac{100}{26} \qquad \frac{63}{20}$$

Decimals

Before trying decimal problems, start by showing a decimal number, such as 5.1248, or 23.87, or 14.47. Ask, "*About* what whole number is this? Is this about halfway between two numbers?" When students are familiar with interpreting individual decimal numbers, pose problems. Ask them to estimate the number of wholes the result is closest to. For example:

$$\begin{array}{r} 5.17 \\ 6.48 \\ + 3.30 \\ \hline \end{array} \qquad 36.89 - 4.11$$

$$3.91 \times 2.1$$

$$42.01 + 7.123 + 0.98$$

Is It Bigger or Smaller?

With any of the suggested types of estimation problem, pose a question about the result to help students focus their estimation. "Is this bigger than 20? Is it smaller than $10.00? If I have $20.00, do I have enough to buy these four things?"

Mentally Checking Calculator Results

Materials: Calculator for each student

Estimation can be used to check an answer obtained with a calculator. Students need to realize how easy and common it is to make mistakes on a calculator, even for people who use calculators all the time. It's very easy to press the wrong number key or the wrong operation. Sometimes we leave out a number by accident, or a sticky key doesn't register. However, people who are good at using the calculator always make a mental estimate so they can tell whether their result is reasonable.

Pose some problems like this one:

> I was adding 212, 357, and 436 on my calculator. The answer I got was 615. Was that a reasonable answer? Why do you think so?

Include problems in which the result is reasonable and problems in which it is not. When the answer is unreasonable, some students might be interested in figuring out what happened. For example, in the above case, the user accidentally entered 46 instead of 436. Here are some other examples:

> Entering 3.46 + 5.18 gave the answer 8.65.
>
> Entering 111 × 8 gave the answer 8,888.
>
> Entering 1.23 × 4 gave the answer 49.2.
>
> Entering 38.7 × 2000 gave the answer 7,740.
>
> Entering 381 + 202 + 17 gave the answer 760.

Number Sense with the Calculator

Materials: Calculator for each student

Give students an "answer" to start with, picking a target number that has many factors, such as 12, 18, 20, 24, 30, 36, or 60. Ask, "What multiplication problems would result in our target number as an answer? Use a calculator to check your ideas." For a target number such as 20, students will probably give some whole-number problems, such as 4×5 or 2×10. Write down their ideas. Then ask if they can think of any problems that would use fractions; for example, $1/3$ of what number is 20? Using the calculator with fractional amounts may lead to approximate numbers. That is, when students type in $1 \div 3 \times 60$ or 0.3333333×60 to see if that gives them 20, the resulting display will be 19.999998. Students should be able to recognize what the exact answer is and record it correctly.

Related Homework Options

Problems with Many Numbers   Students invent a problem with many numbers to be added and subtracted. For example:

$$30 - 6 + 92 - 20 + 56 + 70 + 8$$

Students show how they can reorder the numbers in the problem to make it easier to solve. They solve the problem using two different methods to double-check their solution. One way might be using the calculator. Save students' problems to use in Ten-Minute Math for further practice with estimation and number sense.

Broken Calculator

Students work to make a number appear on their calculator display without using particular keys, which are said to be "broken." The broken keys might be operations, digits, or both. After students find one solution, they create others by making a slight change in the first one. In this way, they establish a pattern.

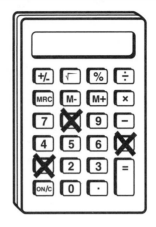

Mathematical Emphasis

Broken Calculator helps students develop flexibility in doing calculations. They pull numbers apart and put them back together in a variety of ways as they look for expressions to substitute for given numbers. The focus is on

Materials
Calculator for each student

- finding alternative paths to an answer when a familiar one isn't available
- finding many ways to get one answer
- writing related computation problems

Procedure

Step 1. Pose the problem. For example, "I want to make 35 using my calculator, but the 3 key and the 5 key are broken. How can I make my calculator display show 35?"

Step 2. Students solve the problem by themselves. They record their solution in some way that another student can understand. Students in small groups check one another's solutions on their calculators.

Step 3. List some of the solutions on the board. For example, here are some possible solutions to making 35 with the 3 and 5 key broken:

$$61 - 26 \qquad 29 + 6 \qquad 4 \times 9 - 1$$

Step 4. Students choose one solution and extend it. In this way, they make a series of related solutions that follows a pattern. As necessary, remind them about which keys are broken.

$61 - 26$	$29 + 6$	$2 \times 18 - 1$
$62 - 27$	$28 + 7$	$4 \times 9 - 1$
$64 - 29$	$27 + 8$	$6 \times 6 - 1$
	$26 + 9$	
	$24 + 11$	

Students check one another's solutions and find another solution that follows the same pattern.

Restricting Digit Keys

Students make numbers without using the digits in those numbers. For example:

Make 1,000 with 1 and 0 broken.

Possible solution and extended pattern:

998 + 2
997 + 3
996 + 4

Here are some other problems of this type:

Make 60 with the 6 and 0 keys broken.

Make 123 with 1, 2, and 3 broken.

Make 55 with 5 broken.

Make 0.25 with 2 and 5 broken.

You could also restrict the choice of operation. For example:

Make 10,000 with 1, 0, and plus (+) broken.

Restricting Operation Keys

Present problems in which the one or more of the operation keys are broken. That is, you might ask students to make a particular number using only addition (the −, ×, and ÷ keys are broken). If you suggest a large number, students can make use of landmark numbers. For example:

Make 2,754 from two or more numbers, using only addition.

Possible solutions and extended patterns:

2,000 + 700 + 54	2,748 + 6
2,000 + 600 + 154	2,749 + 5
2,000 + 500 + 254	2,750 + 4
2,000 + 400 + 354	2,751 + 3

Pose similar problems restricting other operations. For example:

Make 8, using only subtraction (the +, ×, and ÷ keys are broken).

Possible solutions and extended patterns:

20 − 12	1,008 − 1,000
19 − 11	908 − 900
18 − 10	808 − 800
17 − 9	708 − 700

You can also make problems of this type that involve decimal numbers. For example:

> Make 0.25 using only division.

> Make 0.25 using only addition and subtraction.

You could sometimes give problems that allow the use of more than one operation, or a combination of operations. For example:

> Make 24 using only multiplication or division, or both (the + and – keys are broken).

Possible solutions and extended patterns:

1×24	$24 \div 1$	$24 \times 1 \div 1$
2×12	$48 \div 2$	$24 \times 2 \div 2$
3×8	$72 \div 3$	$24 \times 3 \div 3$
4×6		$24 \times 4 \div 4$

(One student filled a page with the third series so he could say he'd gotten the most answers.)

Making Decimals

Students make particular decimal numbers without using the decimal point. This activity should be done only after students have some experience relating decimals to fractions and to division. Start with simple decimals such as 0.1, 0.5, 0.25, 0.75, or 1.5. You might provide a solution or two and challenge them to find some more: "I can make 0.5 on my calculator by using the keys 1 ÷ 2. Why do you think that works? Can you find another way to make 0.5?"

Possible solutions for 0.5:

> $2 \div 4$
> $3 \div 6$
> $4 \div 8$
> $5 \div 10$
> $100 \div 200$
> $1,000 \div 2,000$

Getting to 100 or to 1,000

Students try to make the target number of 100 or 1,000 from a given starting number. They may use any operations or keys they like, except the clear key. For example:

> Start at 54. Try to make 100 without using the clear key.

One possible solution:

> $54 \div 6 \times 10 + 10 = 100$

Here are a few other problems of this type:

Make 100 starting with 7.

Make 100 starting with –125.

Make 1,000 starting with 12,875.

Make 10,000 starting with 3.

You might also limit or restrict certain operation or digit keys, or require that a given number (–150, for example) or operation be used. For example:

Make 100 using only multiplication.

Make 100 using all four operations (+ – × ÷).

Another time, students might look for the route with the least number of steps.

Related Homework Option

Pose one or two Broken Calculator problems. Challenge students to solve the problems in more than one way and to try making a series of solutions that follow a pattern. They write down their solutions, being sure that another student could read them and do them on the calculator.

Students can create solutions even without calculators at home. Give them time to test their solutions on the calculator in school the following day.

Nearest Answer

Given a computation problem and four approximate answers, students pick the closest answer by rounding the numbers in the problem and computing mentally. In a variation, students choose an approximate number for an unknown point on a number line between two labeled points.

$10 \cdots 20$

$$12 \times 17 \approx$$

150
200
250
300

Mathematical Emphasis

Nearest Answer provides practice with estimating answers by rounding numbers for easier mental computation. This kind of thinking is useful for mentally checking answers found by calculator. The focus is on

- approximating numbers
- calculating mentally
- comparing answer choices to find the one closest to the actual answer

Procedure

Preparation. Cut apart the problem strips on the Nearest Answer transparencies. Store each type of problem (whole numbers, decimals, fractions, percents, number lines) in its own envelope.

Step 1. Prepare a problem with four answer choices. Use the Nearest Answer problems provided or design your own. If writing your own, include as one answer a fairly round number that is a good estimate and three other answers that you think might be tempting. For example:

$$2{,}897{,}897 + 37 \approx \quad 5{,}000{,}000 \quad 3{,}000{,}000 \quad 2{,}000{,}000 \quad 29{,}000{,}000$$

Use transparencies if you have an overhead projector, or write problems on the board or chart paper, using a large sheet of paper to cover and uncover them.

Tell students that you are going to show them an arithmetic problem for only a few seconds. They are to round the numbers in the problem to make them easier to compute with, and then estimate the answer.

Step 2. Present the problem, keeping the answers covered, for 20 to 30 seconds. Decrease this time to 15 seconds as students become accustomed to the activity and problem type. It is important not to show the problem so long that students have time to work it out in writing.

Step 3. Uncover the answer choices. Students write down the answer they think is closest. For the example given in step 1, they might approximate the numbers as 3,000,000 + 0, or 2,900,000 + 40, and choose 3,000,000 as the closest answer.

Step 4. Discuss strategies. One or two students tell how they rounded numbers and why they chose the answer they did. The class discusses alternative ways to think about the problem and resolves any disagreements.

Special Note

The Nearest Answer transparency masters offer whole-number problems for the basic activity, plus decimal, fraction, percent, and number line problems for the variations. You can supplement these with problems that you or your students write. In any Nearest Answer session, do only a few problems at a time.

Nearest Answer
Variations

Decimal Problems

Students round the decimals to the nearest whole number or, for large numbers, to a landmark number. For example, they might round 527.9 − 2.1321 to either 528 − 2 or 530 − 0. The accuracy needed will depend on the answer choices.

Fraction and Mixed-Number Problems

Students round the fractions to the nearest whole number (or occasionally to $^1/_2$) and estimate. For example, they could think of $2^5/_8 + ^7/_8$ as close to $2^1/_2 + 1$.

Percent Problems

Students use a nearby familiar percent to help them choose an answer. For example, they could consider 26% of 77 to be close to 25% (or $^1/_4$) of 80.

Number Line Problems

Each of these problems shows a number line with three points labeled, two points with numbers and the third point with the letter A. Students choose the number that is closest to point A. For example:

2	A	5

A is nearest: 3   3.5   4   4.5

Comparing Estimation in Addition and Multiplication

Pose sets of addition and multiplication problems that use the same numbers for their addends and factors. Rather than choosing the "nearest answer," students work in pairs to write four good answer choices for each problem. They will likely find that the answers for addition problems cannot range in size as much as answers for multiplication if they are to be good choices (that is, choices that are tempting for some reason). For example, notice the difference in the range of the following "good choices" for two problems using the same digits but different operations:

$726 + 1{,}177 \approx$	1,800	1,900	2,000	8,300
$726 \times 1{,}177 \approx$	8,400	80,000	700,000	800,000

Rounding Different Factors

Materials: Calculator for each student

Pose multiplication problems without answer choices. Specify that students may round *only one* of the two factors for their calculation. Students use calculators to investigate the possibilities. "Which factor should you round for the closest estimate? By how much can you round and still get a reasonably accurate answer?"

Students will probably find that if the two factors are close in size, rounding either factor has approximately the same effect. For example, with 38×52 ($= 1{,}976$), either 38×50 ($= 1{,}900$) or 40×52 ($= 2{,}080$) will give a reasonable approximation. Some may discover that rounding both factors ($40 \times 50 = 2{,}000$) gives a closer approximation because the numbers are rounded in opposite directions.

If, however, the two factors are of very different size, rounding the larger factor will result in a closer answer than rounding the smaller one. For example, with 8×389 ($= 3{,}112$), rounding to 8×400 ($= 3{,}200$) produces a closer answer than 10×389 ($= 3{,}890$), even though we added only 2 to the 8 whereas we added 11 to the 389.

Related Homework Options

Students Invent Their Own Problems   At home, students prepare problems with four answer choices. They write about how they would think through their own problems. Guide students to use numbers that are near landmark numbers or, in the case of fractions, near whole numbers. In another Ten-Minute Math session, students might exchange their problems with others and compare strategies.

Page of Problems to Do at Home   Students take home two copies of a page with 6–8 problems, each with four answer choices (see page 47 for an example). The second copy is for a family member or friend. Working simultaneously, they make their choices as quickly as they reasonably can without working the problem out in writing. They then take as much time as they need to check their answers, either in writing or with a calculator. This is a good activity when you have introduced a new kind of problem, as you can set up a page designed for in-depth exploration of that problem type.

A.	29 + 52 ≈	40	60	80	100
B.	545 – 240 ≈	200	300	400	700
C.	50,102 – 2,898 ≈	10,000	20,000	40,000	50,000
D.	32,010 – 934 ≈	12,000	23,000	31,000	51,000
E.	36,010 – 19,999 ≈	1,600	16,000	18,000	56,000
F.	5,210 + 298 ≈	5,400	5,500	7,000	8,000
G.	591,000 + 211,000 ≈	700,000	800,000	900,000	10,000,000
H.	3,928,012 – 43 ≈	28,000	350,000	3,000,000	4,000,000
I.	3,051,860 + 815 ≈	5,000,000	4,000,000	3,000,000	2,000,000
J.	7,108 – 141 ≈	5,000	6,000	7,000	8,000
K.	5,982 – 978 ≈	6,000	7,000	14,000	15,000
L.	608 × 980 ≈	5,000	50,000	600,000	690,000
M.	9 × 211 ≈	20	200	2,000	20,000
N.	50,300 ÷ 4,926 ≈	1	10	100	1,000
O.	59 × 11 ≈	60	500	600	6,000

Decimals

A.	$1.1 \times 54 \approx$	5.4	54	540	5,400
B.	$342 + 0.999 \approx$	14,000	13,000	12,000	340
C.	$82 \div 4.2 \approx$	0.5	2	20	40
D.	$24.8 + 3.1 \approx$	28	280	27	270
E.	$498 \times 10.13 \approx$	5.00	50.0	500	5,000
F.	$59.3 \times 1.1 \approx$	60	600	6,000	60,000
G.	$435.4 \div 0.98 \approx$	4.4	44	440	4,400
H.	$268 \div 9.9 \approx$	25	250	2.5	2,500
I.	$402 \times 2.96 \approx$	400	800	1,200	8,000
J.	$25 - 2.1 \approx$	4	12	23	30
K.	$4.3 - 1.412 \approx$	0	1	3	6
L.	$29.93 - 2.1 \approx$	9	20	25	28
M.	$80.5 \div 3.97 \approx$	4	10	20	80
N.	$311 + 3.71 \approx$	11	300	600	800

A.	$8\frac{1}{13} \times 2\frac{9}{11} \approx$	16	18	24	64
B.	$15\frac{7}{8} + 2\frac{6}{7} \approx$	17	18	19	29
C.	$5\frac{9}{11} - 2\frac{7}{8} \approx$	2	3	$3\frac{2}{3}$	32.3
D.	$3\frac{7}{8} + \frac{1}{15} \approx$	3	4	38.23	50
E.	$\frac{32}{66}$ of $22 \approx$	$\frac{1}{3}$	7	10	45
F.	$\frac{1}{3} + \frac{7}{8} \approx$	$\frac{3}{4}$	$\frac{8}{11}$	$\frac{8}{24}$	1.25
G.	$\frac{3}{4}$ of $83 \approx$	20	60	240	560
H.	$\frac{3895}{39} \approx$	0.10	10	100	1,000
I.	$\frac{1}{11} + \frac{8}{9} \approx$	1	2	10	18
J.	$\frac{1}{3} + \frac{4}{7} \approx$	$\frac{1}{2}$	1	2	3
K.	$\frac{11}{4} \approx$	0.5	2.8	15	44
L.	$\frac{5}{9} \times 19 \approx$	2	10	20	100
M.	$\frac{1}{2} \times \frac{5}{17} \approx$	$\frac{10}{17}$	$\frac{1}{8}$	$\frac{2}{8}$	$\frac{5}{8}$

Nearest Answer

A.	33% of 15.85 ≈	5	45	450	500
B.	198% of 15 ≈	7.5	15	30	3,000
C.	51% of 79 ≈	16	35	40	100
D.	98% of 14.3 ≈	1,400	143	14	0.143
E.	25.9% of 774 ≈	0.2	2	20	200
F.	33% of 152 ≈	50	180	450	4,500
G.	73% of 406.2 ≈	50	100	200	300
H.	24% of 83.6 ≈	2	20	27	100
I.	A coat listed at $79.95 is on sale for 20% off the list price. The sale cost is about:	$40	$59.95	$64	$70
J.	A bicycle listed at $210 is on sale at a 30% discount. The sale price is about:	$70	$150	$180	$200
K.	With increase at 8% per year, an article now costing $49.58 may be expected, in 12 months time, to cost about:	$40	$54	$57	$100

Nearest Answer

Number Line

A.

0.7   A   0.8

A is nearest:

0.6   0.15   0.76   0.79

B.

0   A   1

A is nearest:

-1 $\frac{1}{4}$ $\frac{2}{5}$ $\frac{3}{4}$

C.

-3 -1 A

A is nearest:

-5 -2 0   1

D.

2   A   5

A is nearest:

3   3.5   4   4.5

E.

6   A 10

A is nearest:

6   7   8   9

F.

8   A   9

A is nearest:

8.5   8.21   8.36   8.7

G.

800   A 900

A is nearest:

8.6   8.7   840   870

H.

580 A   600

A is nearest:

581   582   585   590

I.

$\frac{1}{2}$ A   1

A is nearest:

$\frac{1}{4}$ $\frac{2}{3}$ $\frac{5}{6}$ $\frac{6}{8}$

Nearest Answer

Circle the answer nearest to the exact answer.

A. 38 + 49 ≈   70   80   90   100

B. 795 − 202 ≈   400   500   600   700

C. 10 × 312 ≈   300   2,000   3,000   20,000

D. 26 × 8 ≈   100   200   300   400

E. 250 ÷ 8 ≈   15   30   300   2,000

F. $\frac{1}{2}$ × 39 ≈   20   30   40   80

G. $\frac{9}{10}$ + $\frac{1}{13}$ ≈   0   1   2   3

H.

42 A   46   A is nearest:

$42\frac{1}{4}$ 43   45   47

Ten-Minute Math   47

Activities for Data and Probability

The data activities in this section provide opportunities for students to collect, represent, describe, and interpret data in a meaningful way. Students work largely with data they gather themselves, and they have many chances to develop their own ways of representing those data. They approach graphing as a way to tell a story about a set of data and as a basis for posing new questions and making predictions. Through the probability activities, students make judgments about the likelihood of real events as well as the likelihood of drawing a particular color mix from a collection of objects of two colors.

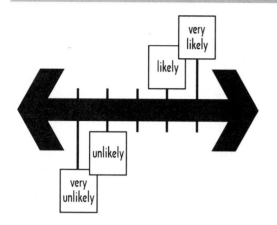

Students think about events in the world around them, considering which events are likely and which are unlikely to occur. They sort statements about events into the two categories "Likely" and "Unlikely." As they become familiar with these ideas, adding the categories "Very Likely" and "Very Unlikely" encourages students to make finer distinctions about the probability of these events. Students can also decide whether one event is more likely or less likely than another.

Materials
Collection of statements naming events that are likely or unlikely

Mathematical Emphasis

Likely or Unlikely? involves students in considering the likelihood of the occurrence of a particular event. Ideas about probability are notoriously difficult for children and adults. In the early and middle elementary grades, we simply want students to examine familiar events in order to judge how likely or unlikely they are. The focus is on

- describing events with terms such as *likely, unlikely, more likely*, and *less likely*
- deciding what sorts of events in our lives are more and less likely

Procedure

Preparation. The first time you do this activity, prepare some statements ahead of time. For subsequent sessions, students can write *likely/unlikely* statements at home, as they arrive in class, or as part of the Ten-Minute Math session. Occasionally you might ask just a few students to prepare some statements ahead. To ensure a balanced supply, ask each student to write two statements, one likely and one unlikely. Each statement should be written on a strip of paper that can be taped to a posted chart.

Step 1. Start a chart with two headings, *Likely* and *Unlikely*. The first time you present the activity, discuss with students what these words mean and what kinds of things are likely and unlikely.

Step 2. Read, one at a time, statements of events that are likely or unlikely to occur. Be sure each statement is written on a separate strip of paper. Following are some ideas to start with. The likelihood of some of these events is, of course, related to the characteristics of your community, the season, and so forth.

> One hundred cars will pass our school during the day today.
>
> An airplane will land on our school roof today.
>
> Half of the students in our school will stay home with colds tomorrow.

A few students will stay home with colds tomorrow.

The school cafeteria will be noisy today.

Fewer than 20 people in [name of your community] will order a pizza today.

It will snow here tomorrow.

It will rain here sometime in the next two weeks.

Scientists will discover that the earth is flat.

Our class will get five new students before the end of the year.

Step 3. Students decide whether each event is likely or unlikely. After some discussion, tape the statement strip on the chart under the appropriate heading. Because there will not be enough time to discuss a statement from everyone in the class, select a few and save the rest for the next Likely or Unlikely? session. You can keep the chart posted in the classroom and add new statements each time you do the activity.

Adding More Categories

After students have had some experience with the ideas of likely and unlikely, ask them to write some statements that are *very likely* or *very unlikely*. Discuss: "How is a statement that is *very unlikely* different from one that is just *unlikely?* How is a statement that is *very likely* different from one that is just *likely?* How many of the statements already on our chart fit into these new categories? Can you think of a way to change a *likely* statement into a *very likely* statement?"

Note that in these activities, it's better to avoid the categories *certain* or *impossible* because students of this age can get into endless arguments about whether it's indeed *certain* that the sun will rise tomorrow, or whether it's genuinely *impossible* that a large white rabbit will serve lunch in the school cafeteria today.

Changing Likely to Unlikely

Looking at your lists of likely and unlikely statements, students choose one statement and change it in such a way that it would move to the opposite list. For example:

Unlikely: An airplane will land on our school roof tomorrow.

Change to likely: An airplane will not land on our school roof tomorrow.

Likely: The school cafeteria will be noisy today.

Change to unlikely: The school cafeteria will be quiet today.

Choose a few of these to discuss. Do other students agree that the statement that was at first likely is now unlikely?

More or Less Likely?

Introduce the element of comparison with statements using *more likely* or *less likely.* For example:

> It is more likely that it will rain tomorrow than that it will snow.

> It is less likely that I will see a mouse on the way home than that I will see a dog.

As you or the students suggest such statements, discuss them. Does everyone agree with them?

Related Homework Options

Writing Likely/Unlikely Statements   At home, students write statements to bring in for sorting during the next Likely or Unlikely? session. You may want to provide a homework sheet with two sentences to be filled in:

> It is likely that _____.
>
> It is unlikely that _____.

After students have some experience with these ideas, you can add other sentences that make finer distinctions or comparisons:

> It is very likely that _____.
>
> It is very unlikely that _____.
>
> It is more likely/less likely that _____ than that _____.

Connections with the Community   Students might write statements of likely or unlikely events that occur in their community. For example, they might consider statements like these:

> The river will flood this year.
>
> In a few years, we will have less polluted air in our city.
>
> The trash in the park will be cleaned up by next Sunday.
>
> The new school addition will be finished by September.

They may need to interview people who know about these events to help them decide whether each is likely or unlikely. They may even be able to set into motion actions that could change the probability of some event, such as organizing a park cleanup.

Exploring Data

Students choose something to observe about themselves. Once the question is determined, you quickly graph the data on the board or chart paper as students give their individual answers. The graph can be done as a line plot, a list, a table, or a bar graph. Students describe what they can tell from the data, generate some new questions, and, if appropriate, make predictions about what will happen the next time they collect the same data.

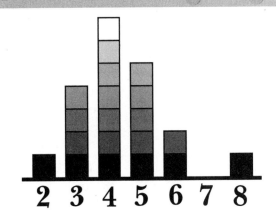

Mathematical Emphasis

Exploring Data gives students many quick opportunities to collect, graph, describe, and interpret data about themselves and the world around them. The focus is on

Materials
Chart paper and marking pens

• describing important features of the data
• interpreting and posing questions about the data

Procedure

Step 1. Choose a question. So that the data can be determined on the spot, make sure the question involves data that students already know or can observe: How many buttons are you wearing today? What month is your birthday? What is the best thing you ate yesterday? Are you wearing shoes or sneakers or sandals? How did you get to school today? What is your favorite fruit? What do you usually eat for breakfast?

Step 2. Quickly collect and display the data. Use a list, a table, a line plot, or a bar graph. For example, a line plot for how many buttons students are wearing could look something like this:

```
                X
    X           X           X
    X           X           X
    X           X       X   X           X
    X           X       X   X           X
    X       X   X       X   X       X   X
    0       1   2       3   4       5   6
           Number of Buttons
```

Step 3. Ask students to describe the data. What do they notice about it? For data that have a numerical order (How many buttons do you have today? How many people live in your house? How many months until your birthday?), ask questions like these:

"Are the data spread out or close together? What is the highest and lowest value? Where do most of the data seem to fall? What seems typical or usual for this class?"

For data in categories (What is your favorite kind of book? How do you get to school? What month is your birthday?), ask questions like these: "Which categories have a lot of data? few data? none? Is there a way to categorize the data differently to get other information?"

Step 4. Ask students to interpret and predict. "Why do you think that the data came out this way? Does anything about the data surprise you? Do you think we'd get similar data if we asked the same question tomorrow? next week? in another class? with adults?"

Step 5. List any new questions. Keep a running list of questions you can use for further data collection and analysis. You may want to ask some of the same questions again.

Exploring Data Variations

Categories

If students take surveys about "favorites"—flavor of ice cream, breakfast cereal, book, color—or other data that fall into categories, the graphs are often flat and uninteresting because you get too many different categories. There is not too much to say, for example, about a graph like this:

```
X
X                X
X       X        X        X
X       X        X        X                 X
X       X        X        X        X        X        X
Vanilla Chocolate Rocky   Chocolate Cookies  Vanilla  Strawberry
                  Road    Chip     'n' Cream Fudge
```

It is more interesting for students to group their results into fewer, more descriptive categories, so that they can see other things about the data. In this case, even though vanilla seems to be the "favorite" with the most entries, another way of grouping the data seems to show that flavors with some chocolate in them are really the favorites.

Chocolate flavors ╫╫ ╫╫ |||

Flavors without chocolate ╫╫ |

Data from Home

For homework, students collect data that involves asking questions or making observations at home: What time do your brothers and sisters go to bed? How many states (or how many countries) have you visited? How many cousins do you have? They bring in their answers to use in the class activity.

Data from Another Class or from Teachers

Depending on your school situation, you may be able to assign students to collect data from other classrooms or from teachers. Students are always interested in surveying others about questions that interest them, such as this one for teachers: "When you were little, what did you like best about school?"

Familiar Fractions

Once the class has their data grouped into two or three categories, students can write the proportions as fractions, and then relate these to familiar fractions and percents to describe the amounts in "round" numbers, which are often more meaningful. For example, in the ice-cream flavors survey, $6/19$ of the class prefers flavors without chocolate. This is less than half. It is about a third since $6/18$ is a third. Nineteenths are smaller than eighteenths, so it's less than $33\frac{1}{3}\%$, maybe about 30–32%. Students can use the calculator to check their estimates.

What Is Likely?

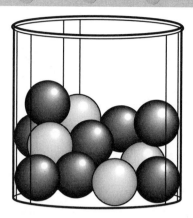

Given a clear container filled with objects of two different colors, students predict whether a random drawing of 10 objects will give them more of one color or the other. They blindly draw out 10 objects, one at a time, then record the color and replace each object before picking the next one. Students compare their expectations with their actual results before repeating with a second sample of 10 objects.

Materials

Clear container, such as a fishbowl or large glass or plastic jar

Objects that are all very similar in size and shape, but come in two colors (such as cubes, beans, beads, marbles)

Mathematical Emphasis

What Is Likely? involves students in thinking about ratio and proportion and in considering the likelihood of the occurrence of a particular event. Ideas about probability are notoriously difficult for both children and adults. In the early and middle elementary grades, we simply want students to examine familiar events in order to judge how likely or unlikely they are. In this activity, the focus is on

- visualizing the ratio of two colors in a collection
- making predictions and comparing predictions with outcomes
- exploring the relationship between a sample and the group of objects from which it comes

Procedure

Step 1. Fill the container with objects of two colors. When you first do this activity, put much more of one color into the container. For example, with every 10 cubes, you might have 9 yellow and 1 red. Thus, if you used 40 cubes, 36 would be yellow and 4 would be red. Mix these well inside the container. Continue to use markedly different proportions for a while.

Step 2. Students predict which color will occur most often if they draw out 10 objects. Carry the container around the room so that everyone can get a good look at its contents. Then ask students to make their predictions. "What is likely to happen if we pull out 10 objects? Will we get more yellows or more reds? Will we get a lot more of one color than the other? About how many of each will we get?"

Step 3. Students draw 10 objects, replacing them after each draw. Ask a student, with eyes closed, to draw out one object. Record its color on the board before the student puts the object back. Nine more students do them same. Use tallies to record the colors students pull out. For example:

Red ~~||||~~ ||| **Yellow** ||

Step 4. Discuss what happened. "Is this about what you expected? Why or why not?" With a 9:1 ratio of the two colors, students won't always draw out a sample that is exactly 9 of one color and 1 of the other. Eight red and 2 yellow or 10 red and 0 yellow would also be likely samples. Ask students whether their results are likely or unlikely, given what they can see in the container. What result would be *unlikely,* or surprising? (Of course, surprises can happen, too—just not very often.)

Step 5. Try it again. Students are usually eager to draw another 10 objects to see what happens. "Do you think it's likely that we'll get mostly reds again? Why? About how many do you think we'll get?" Draw objects, tally their colors, and discuss in the same way.

Different Color Mixes

Try a 3:1 ratio, filling the container with 3 of one color for every 1 of the other color. Also try an equal amount of the two colors.

Different Objects

Try using different objects with the same proportion of colors. Does a change like this affect the outcome?

The Whole Class Picks

See what happens when each student in the class draws (and then replaces) one object. Before you start, ask, "If all of us pick an object, about how many reds do you think we'll get? Is it more likely you'll pick a red or a yellow? A *little* more likely or *a lot* more likely?"

Students Fill the Container

Ask students to determine the proportions of each color to put in the container. Set a goal. For example:

> How can we fill the container so that's it's *very likely* we'll get mostly reds when we draw 10?

> How can we fill the container so that it's *unlikely* we'll get more than one red?

> How can we fill the container so that we'll get close to the same number of reds and yellows when we draw 10?

After students decide how to fill the container, proceed with the usual drawing to test their predictions.

Three Colors

Put an equal number of two colors (say, red and yellow) in the container, and mix in many more or many fewer of a third color (blue). "If 10 people pick, about how many of each color do you think we will get? Do you think we'll get the same number of red and yellow, or do you think we will get more of one than the other?"

Using Percents

When predicting what is likely, ask students to state their predictions as percents. For example, "I think it will be about 25% yellow and 75% red." They then express the actual results as percents, and discuss in step 4 what percents would be unlikely or surprising.

Guess My Rule

In this classification game, students try to figure out, through careful observation and questioning, what characteristic a group of things have in common. The leader secretly establishes a "rule," for example, one that describes certain trees, such as "evergreen." The leader then identifies specific items that do and do not fit the rule. Students use this evidence to form hypotheses, then systematically make guesses in order to deduce the rule.

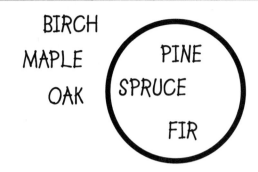

Mathematical Emphasis

Guess My Rule involves students in logical reasoning about the common properties of things that follow a given rule. In the variations, students investigate aspects of number theory and geometry as they learn to recognize and describe the attributes of people, numbers, and two-dimensional geometric shapes. The focus is on

- using evidence to formulate hypotheses
- systematically eliminating possibilities
- formulating questions to logically eliminate possible solutions
- learning to use mathematical terms that describe numbers (for Guess My Rule with Numbers variation)
- recognizing relationships among two-dimensional geometric shapes (for Guess My Rule with Shapes variation)

Materials
Scrap paper (optional, for recording students' guesses)

Procedure

Preparation. As necessary, precede this activity with some discussion of classification, or the different ways things "go together." You might draw on information you have been studying in other curricular areas, such as language arts, science, and social studies.

Step 1. Choose a rule without revealing it and give a few examples.
Announce that you have chosen a "mystery rule." For example, you might start with a rule that describes certain kinds of words. Draw a circle on the board, and explain that every word you place *inside* of the circle follows your rule. If you place a word outside of the circle, that word does *not* follow your rule. Start off by placing a few examples both inside and outside the circle.

For example, suppose your rule is ADJECTIVES. You might start out like this:

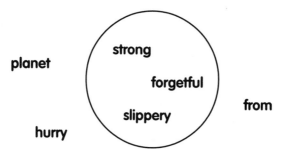

Step 2. Students work to discover your rule. Emphasize that no one is to guess the rule out loud. After considering silently what the rule might be, students test their hypotheses by offering suggestions for other items that might fit the rule. Whether or not you place these suggestions where they expect, students can use this information to eliminate possibilities, devise new solutions, and revise their idea of what the rule might be.

Step 3. Record all suggested solutions. When many of the students seem to have a good idea about the rule, make a list of their ideas. To get responses from everyone, ask the students to record their solutions on scraps of paper and hold them up on a given signal. List all proposed rules on the board. Students may challenge any rules they think don't fit all the clues, giving reasons for their challenges.

Step 4. Invite students to ask further questions. If more than one solution still fits all the clues, students continue to offer examples until only one rule remains. Encourage students to ask questions that eliminate more than one of the proposed solutions.

Guess My Rule with People

People might be classified according to their gender, according to their hair color, according to how they get to school, according to what they are wearing on a given day, and so on. Choose a visually obvious rule that describes some students in the classroom, such as BROWN HAIR, WEARING RED, or WEARING A WATCH. In this version of the activity, it helps to have people who fit the rule stand at one side of the room and those who do not fit the rule stand at the other side.

Once students guess your rule, you might ask them to figure out what fraction of the class fits the rule and what fraction does not, and to find familiar fractions for the numbers they discover (for example, 9 out of 29 students wore red today; that's about one-third).

Guess My Rule with Numbers

Choose a rule that describes a number characteristic. For example, your rule might be that all the numbers you write in the circle are TWO-DIGIT NUMBERS.

During the year, vary this game to include mathematical terms that have come up in class. For example, include factors, multiples, square numbers, prime numbers, odd and even numbers, and *less than* and *more than* concepts. For example, here are some possible rules:

> FACTORS OF 24
>
> MULTIPLES OF 5
>
> PRIME NUMBERS
>
> SQUARE NUMBERS
>
> ODD NUMBERS
>
> NUMBERS LESS THAN 50

Challenge students to test numbers greater than 100 or even greater than 1,000 and see if those numbers are placed where they expect.

Guess My Rule with Shapes

Materials: Transparencies of triangles, quadrilaterals, and other shapes (masters provided on pp. 64–66), and an overhead projector (optional)

Choose a rule that focuses on properties of geometric shapes. You can use an overhead projector with the transparencies provided for triangles, quadrilaterals, and other shapes, or you might draw shapes yourself at the board. For example, here are some possible rules for shapes:

> RIGHT TRIANGLES
>
> EQUILATERAL TRIANGLES
>
> QUADRILATERALS THAT ARE NOT SQUARES
>
> SHAPES WITH MORE THAN FIVE SIDES
>
> SHAPES WITH AT LEAST ONE SET OF PARALLEL SIDES
>
> SHAPES WITH AT LEAST ONE RIGHT ANGLE

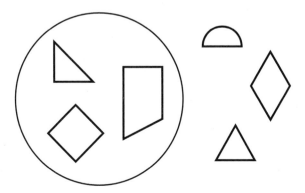

Guess My Rule with Two Rules

When you first play Guess My Rule with two rules, choose rules for which there is no overlap (for example, TRIANGLES and SQUARES). Set up two circles side by side and sort shapes into these circles until students can identify the rules.

When students have had some experience with thinking about two rules at once, choose two rules with some items that fit both categories. For example, using numbers, the rules might be ODD NUMBERS and MULTIPLES OF 3. Demonstrate the use of overlapping circles, with items that fit both rules being placed in the overlapping space that is inside both circles.

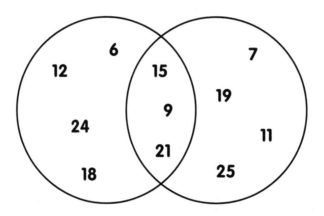

Guess My Rule with Number Pairs

Many teachers first heard the title "Guess My Rule" applied to this version, introduced by Bob Davis in the 1960s. Given a two-column table of numbers, students think of a rule that describes how to operate on the first number to make the second. For example:

a. □	△	b. □	△	c. □	△	d. □	△
7	2	2	6	5	12	1	1
2	–3	4	12	0	2	2	4
9	4	–3	–9	10	22	3	9
6		1		–2	–2	10	

The rules for these tables are (a) subtract 5 from the first number; (b) multiply the first number by 3; (c) double the number and add 2; (d) square the number.

Start by providing two or three number pairs based on your rule. As in the basic activity, students are not to say the rule out loud, but if they think they know the rule, they can tell you a new number pair that fits it. To prompt students, suggest a first number and ask what the second number in the pair would be. Collect and write down any suggestions of number pairs that work until you think many students have figured out the rule. Then ask what the rule is. Students may describe the rule in several different ways; list all the different wordings. Ask if anyone can suggest how the rule might be written as an equation. As needed, model one of their rules with an equation. For example, doubling $\square$ and adding 2 could be written as $2\,(\square) + 2 = \triangle$.

Related Homework Options

Guess My Rule Homework   Prepare a sheet with one Guess My Rule problem for students to work on at home. Try to give examples that could reflect several possible rules. For example, a circle with 5, 15, and 25 inside could be ODD NUMBERS, MULTIPLES OF 5, or FACTORS OF 75. Ask students to find as many different rules as they can that fit the examples given.

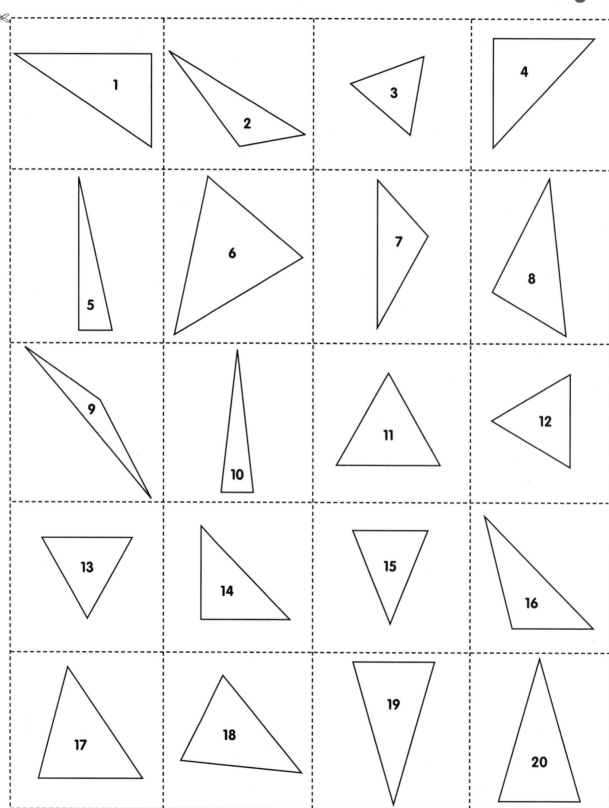

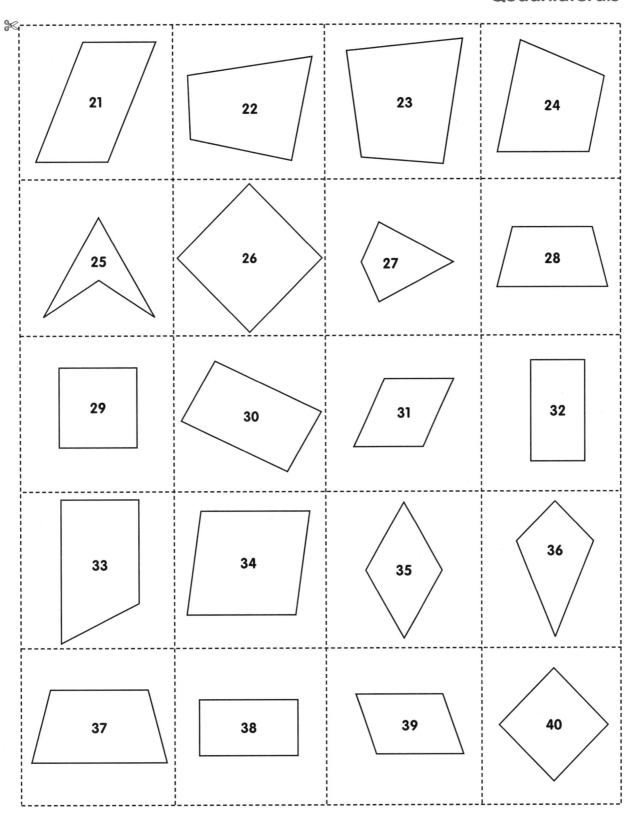

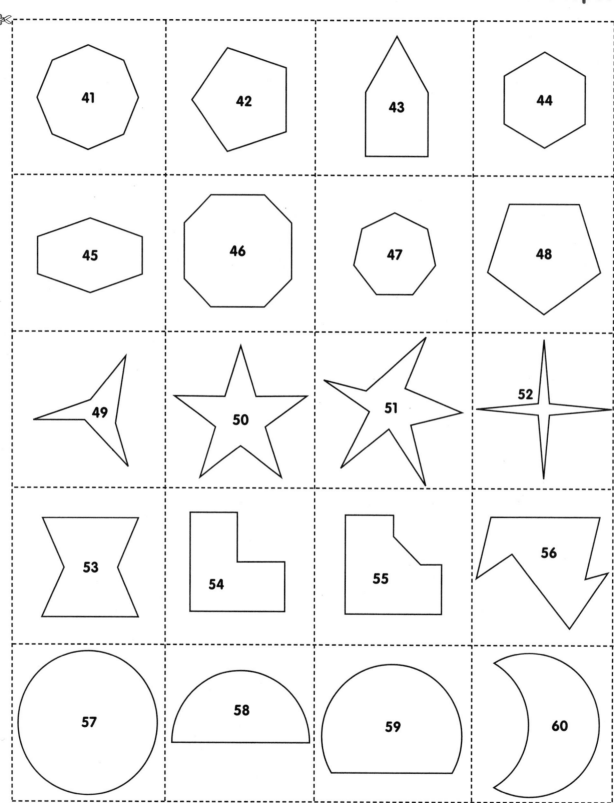

Graph Stories

Students look at a graph shape that shows something changing over time. They imagine what the changing quality might be (for example, height, population, speed, quantity, price, distance, hunger, light) and tell a story about change that fits the graph.

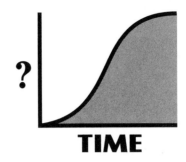

Mathematical Emphasis

This activity is connected to work in the grade 4 and 5 *Investigations* units, *Changes Over Time* and *Patterns of Change*. The graphs that students consider are *qualitative* rather than quantitative. Without numbers on either axis, students must interpret qualities of the shape: relative heights, steepness of slope, pointed or gradual turns, lines going up or going down. The focus is on

- attending to important features of a graph
- imagining the stories behind graphs that show change over time
- drawing a graph to fit a particular story

Materials

Overhead projector

Graph Shapes transparencies (masters provided on pp. 71–72), cut apart

Procedure

Step 1. Show a graph on the overhead. Choose one of the graphs provided or one that you or a student drew. Ask questions to start students thinking: "What could be happening in this graph? What could be changing as time goes by? What might be growing and shrinking? going faster or slower? becoming more or less?" For example:

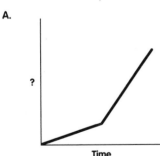

Suppose graph A shows the money in your piggy bank. What is happening? What changes? Why might it change?

Suppose graph A shows the distance traveled as someone walks to school. What happens? Why does the line change direction after about half the time has passed? Does the speed change? In what way? Why might it change?

Step 2. Students talk in pairs about stories that might fit the graph. They might each invent one story, sharing it to be sure it makes sense to another person, or partners might collaborate on a single story. In their story, they tell what variable is being shown and how it changes.

Step 3. Share and discuss the invented stories. A few students tell their stories, explaining or showing how the story fits the shape. There are many possibilities. For example:

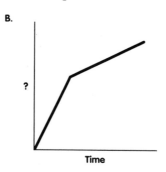

B.

Graph B might show the paint coverage of a house: "At first two painters were working on the house and the work was going quickly, but then one painter left and the other one kept working alone."

Graph B might show the money earned from a spaghetti feed: "The dinner started at 5 o'clock and lot of people came during the first hour so we sold a lot right at the beginning, but then people continued to come slowly over the next couple of hours."

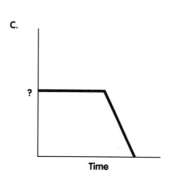

C.

Graph C might show how much sunlight there was: "There was a lot of sunshine in the room. Then later in the afternoon, storm clouds covered the sun and the room got darker and darker until it was night."

Graph C might show how many people: "A lot of people were in the museum for a long time. Suddenly people started leaving and kept leaving until there was no one left."

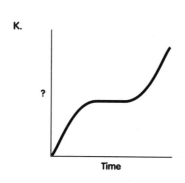

K.

Graph K might show the size of a woodpile: "We cut and stacked firewood most of the morning, but in the middle we took a break to have a snack."

Graph K might show the position of a car on a rural highway: "I was driving along when I suddenly had to stop for a mother raccoon taking her babies across the road. When they were all safely across, I resumed my trip."

Graphs of Personal Change

On a topic you select, students draw a graph of their changing feelings. Here are some ideas for topics:

How awake I feel as I go through a day.

How much I have liked school since the beginning of the year.

How hungry I feel as I go through the day.

How I have felt about math over my years at school.

How my skill at (playing an instrument, playing a sport, reading, drawing, or the like) has changed over the years.

The length of my hair over the past year.

Comparing Stories for Two Graphs

Draw two graphs on the same grid. Students tell stories about the graphs to bring out the similarities and differences. For example:

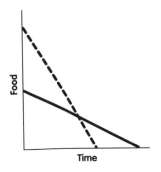

"This is the food in our dogs' dishes at meal-time. The dotted line is the food in Muffin's dish. She gets more food and eats it superfast. The plain line is the food in Max's dish. He eats slowly and we have to keep Muffin from pushing him away and getting her nose in his dish."

Related Homework Options

Making Up Stories   Students take home a graph shape and write one or more stories to go with it.

Inventing Graphs and Stories That Go Together   Students write brief stories of something changing and make a graph to go with it. You might use some of these stories for the variation "Making Graphs for Stories."

Making Graphs for Stories

Materials: Squares of blank transparency film for students

Prepare (or ask a student to prepare) a story about something that change
time. Have in mind a graph that fits the story. Tell the story or write it ou
project it on the overhead for the class to read. Students draw graph shap
fit the story, perhaps on pieces of transparency so they can easily be share
label the changing variable on the vertical axis. Students then discuss the
first in small groups and then with the whole class.

Contrasting Graph Pairs

Show students pairs of graphs. The challenge is to think of a single situatic
explain the difference in the stories told by the two graphs.

In the following pair, for example, both graphs could be telling the story of
someone tossing a ball, tracking the distance of the ball from its starting po
In graph G, the ball is thrown straight upward; it gradually slows down, sto
and returns, picking up speed as it falls. In graph H, the ball is thrown again
wall and bounces straight back.

G.

H.

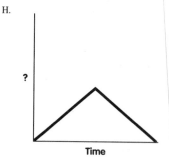

As another example, graphs I and J could both be telling the story of a train
going at a steady speed, but the variable would differ. In graph I, the variable i
the speed; the graph shows the train proceeding at a steady rate. In graph J, the
variable is the position of the train; the graph shows the train progressing stead
ly toward its destination.

I.

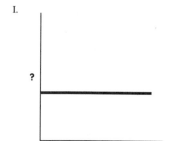

J.

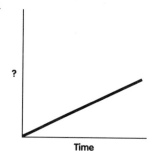

A.

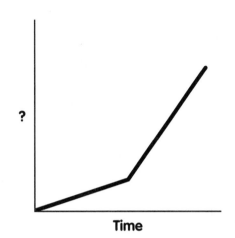

? Time

B.

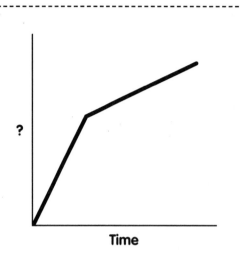

? Time

C.

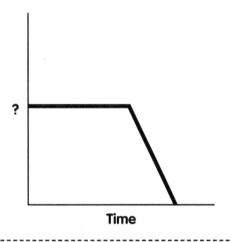

? Time

D.

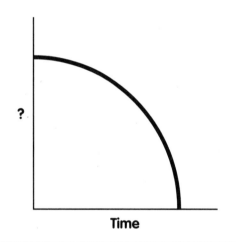

? Time

E.

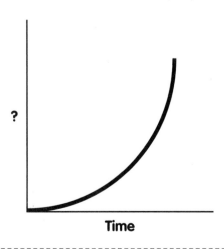

? Time

F.

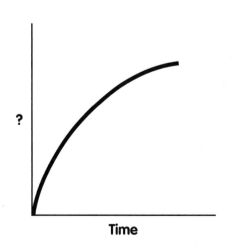

? Time

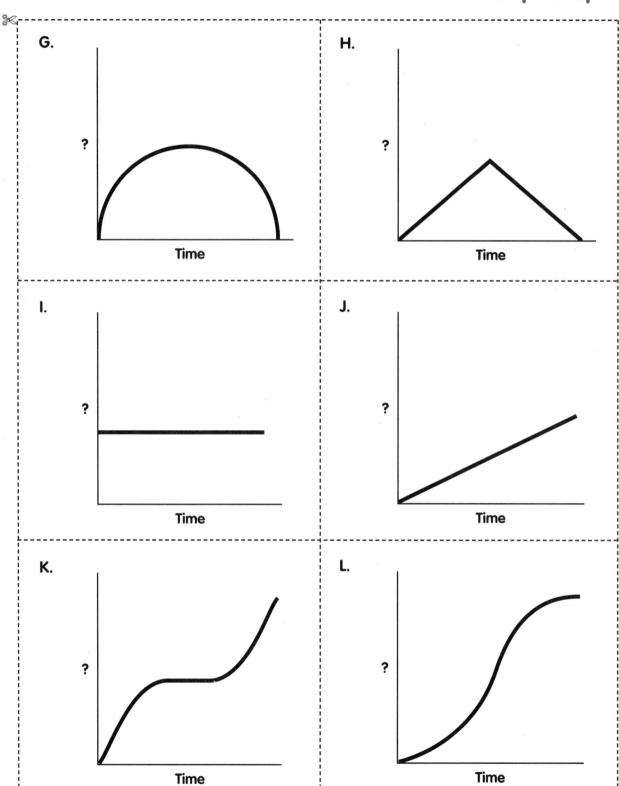

Activities for Geometry and Shape

The activities in this section help students develop an understanding of two- and three-dimensional geometric shapes and the relationships among such shapes. Students form and manipulate mental images of geometric shapes in addition to drawing or otherwise constructing them. Geometric vocabulary emerges naturally as students share and compare their solutions, their creations, and their strategies.

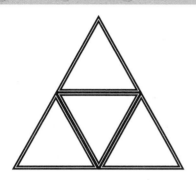

Students briefly view a geometric figure or design. Depending on the kind of figure, they either draw it or build it from the mental image they formed during the brief viewing. Suggested images include 2-D geometric designs, 3-D cube constructions, arrangements of tangram or pattern block pieces, and dot patterns.

Materials

Overhead projector

Quick Images transparencies (masters provided on pp. 77–84)

Mathematical Emphasis

In Quick Images, as students look for meaningful ways to see each image, they may see it as a whole ("a box, three cubes long and two cubes high"), decompose it into memorable parts ("four triangles, pointing up, down, up, down"), or use their knowledge of number relationships to remember a pattern ("4 groups of 5 dots, so it's 20"). The focus is on

- organizing and analyzing visual images
- developing concepts and language needed to reflect on and communicate about spatial relationships
- using geometric vocabulary to describe shapes and patterns
- using number relationships to describe patterns

Procedure

Preparation. Cut apart the figures on the Quick Images transparencies. Keep the identification number with each figure, because it will help you orient the figure on the overhead. Store each type of figure (2-D designs, cubes, dot patterns) in its own envelope. You can supplement these with your own examples or make up other types.

When presenting the activity, be sure that all students are seated facing the overhead screen and have a clear view. You may be able to show two or three Quick Images in a 10-minute session. Some teachers find it valuable to repeat, on successive days, images that they have previously presented.

Step 1. Flash an image for 3 seconds. It's important to show the figure for as close to 3 seconds as possible. If you show it too long, students will draw or build from the figure rather than from their mental image of it; if you show it too briefly, they will not have sufficient time to form a mental image. Students will quickly learn to study the figure carefully while it is visible so they can draw or build it from their mental image.

Step 2. Students draw or build what they saw. Give students a few minutes with the relevant materials (paper and pencil, cubes, tangrams, pattern blocks) to draw or construct a figure that matches the mental image they have formed. When you see that most students have finished working, go on to step 3.

Step 3. Flash the image again, for revision. After showing the image for another 3 seconds, students revise their drawing or building according to what they see in this second viewing. It is essential to provide enough time here, before a third showing, for most students to complete their attempts at drawing or building. While they may not have completed their figure, they should have done all they can do until they see the image displayed again. When student work subsides, go on to step 4.

Step 4. Show the image a third and final time. This time leave the image visible so that all students can complete or revise their solutions.

Step 5. Discuss the mental images students formed. Students share the different ways they saw the figure as they looked at it on successive "flashes."

2-D Geometric Designs

Materials: Transparencies of 2-D geometric designs, paper and pencil

To do the activity with 2-D designs, students need paper and pencil to draw the images they see. When talking about what they saw in successive flashes, many students will say things like "I saw four triangles in a row." You might suggest this strategy for students having difficulty: "Each design is made from familiar geometric shapes. Find these shapes and try to figure out how they are put together."

As students describe their figures, you can introduce the correct geometric terms for component shapes. As you use these terms naturally in class discussion, students too will begin to recognize and use them.

3-D Cubes

Materials: Transparencies of 3-D cube constructions, and Snap™ cubes or other interlocking cubes that connect on all sides (15–20 for each student)

For this version, students need 15–20 interlocking cubes to build the constructions they see. Several of the Quick Images cube figures provided are intentionally ambiguous as some unseen cubes "in the back" may or may not be part of the figure. Students with differing solutions should have the chance to compare and defend their constructions.

Tangrams or Pattern Blocks

Materials: Transparent overhead tangrams or pattern blocks (optional); a set of tangrams for each student or pair; a set of pattern blocks for small groups to share; or paper and pencil

Use a set of transparent overhead tangrams or pattern blocks if you have them. Otherwise, use a regular set and leave small spaces between the pieces as you create a design. Arrange three or four of the shapes on the overhead to form a larger shape or design. Students use their own set of tangrams or pattern blocks to form the image, or they draw the figure. As with 2-D figures, you can introduce correct geometric terms when students describe their figures.

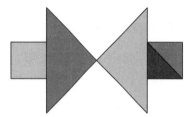

For more challenge, construct a figure using more pieces. Or, continue to use only a few shapes, but leave no spaces between them; this option may result in several different solutions for the same design.

Dot Patterns

Materials: Transparencies of dot patterns, paper and pencil

With dot patterns, students need paper and pencil to draw the patterns. They also have a second task: to figure out how many dots they saw. When students do only one of the tasks, remind them to do the other as well. You will likely see different students using different strategies. For example, some might see a pattern in terms of a multiplication problem, say 6×3, and may not think to draw the dots unless asked. Others will draw the pattern of dots first, *then* figure out how many there are.

Related Homework Options

Creating Quick Images   Students can make up their own Quick Images to challenge the rest of the class. Talk with students about keeping these reasonable—challenging, but not overwhelming. If the images shown are too complex and difficult to remember, other students will just become frustrated.

Family Quick Images   Send images home for students to try with their families. Help them practice the routine first: They show a picture for three seconds; turn it over or cover it while family members try to draw it, then show it again, and so forth. Other family members may be interested in creating their own images for the child to try.

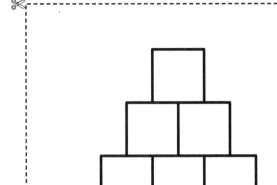

1.

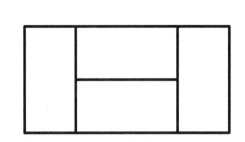

2.

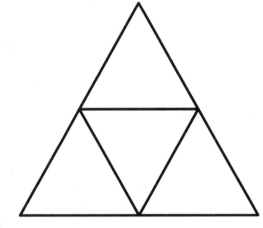

3.

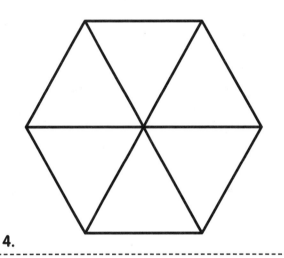

4.

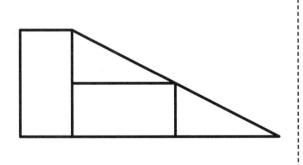

5.

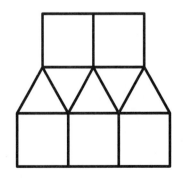

6.

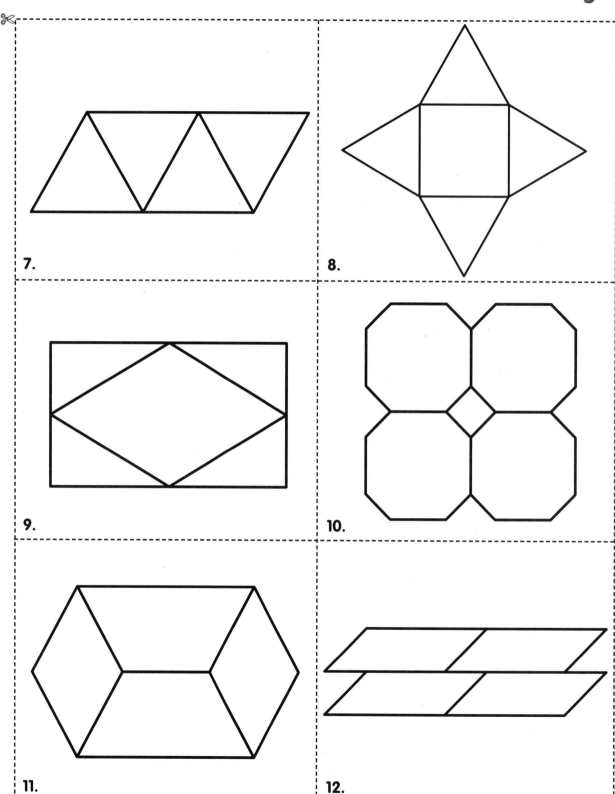

7.

8.

9.

10.

11.

12.

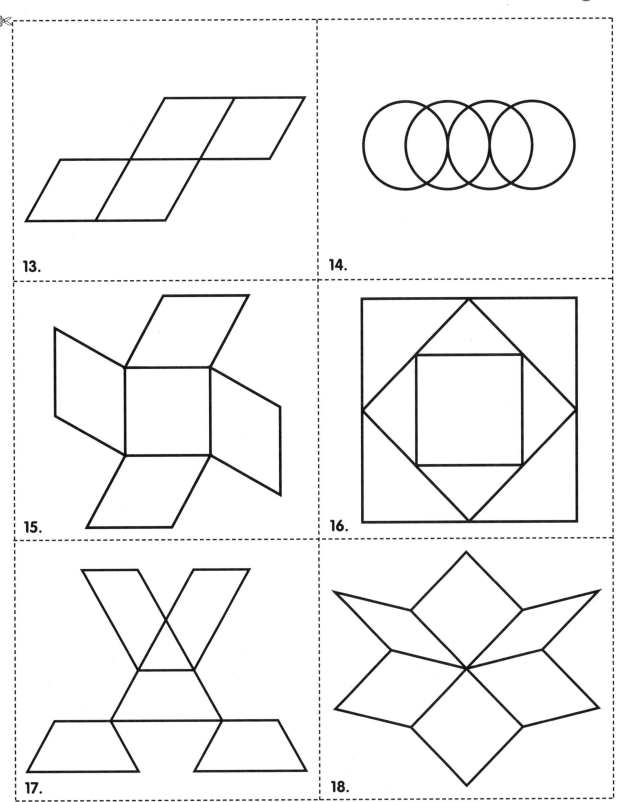

13.

14.

15.

16.

17.

18.

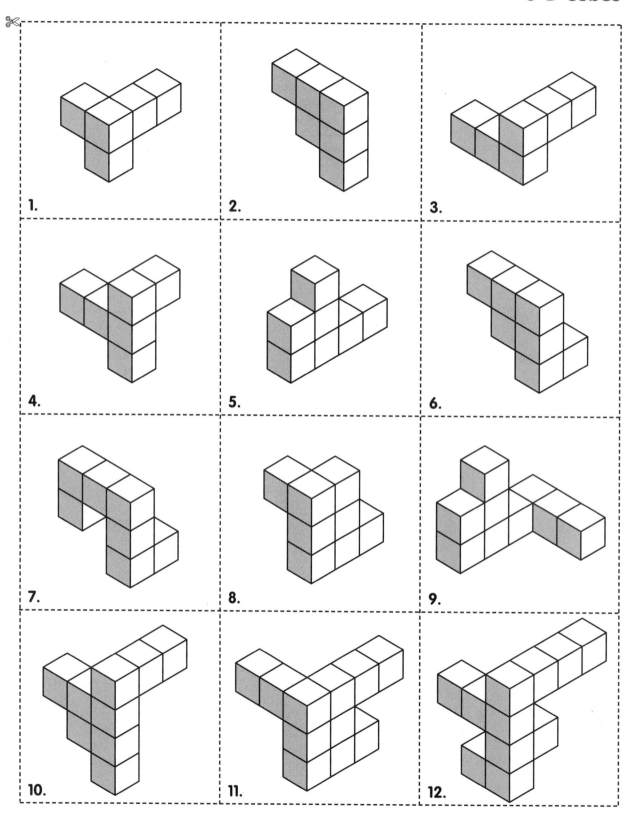

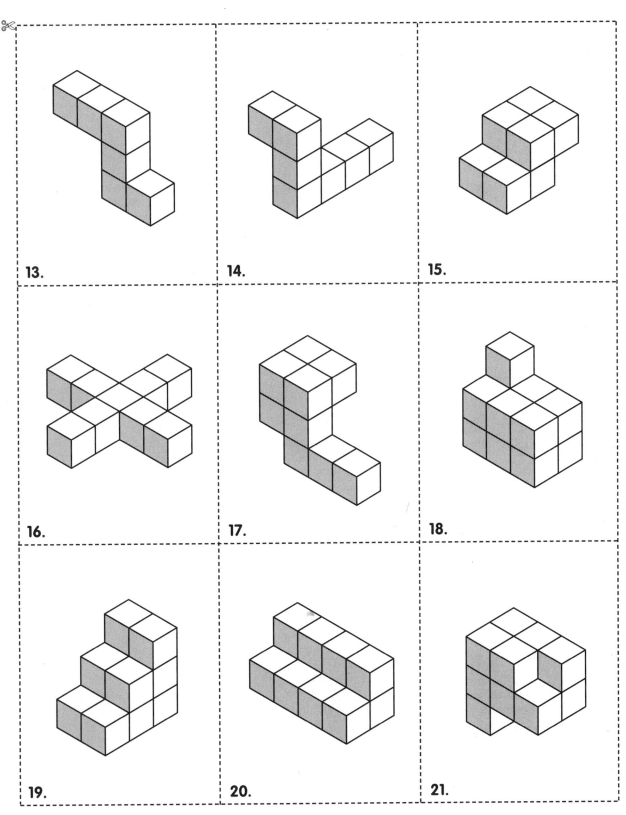

13.

14.

15.

16.

17.

18.

19.

20.

21.

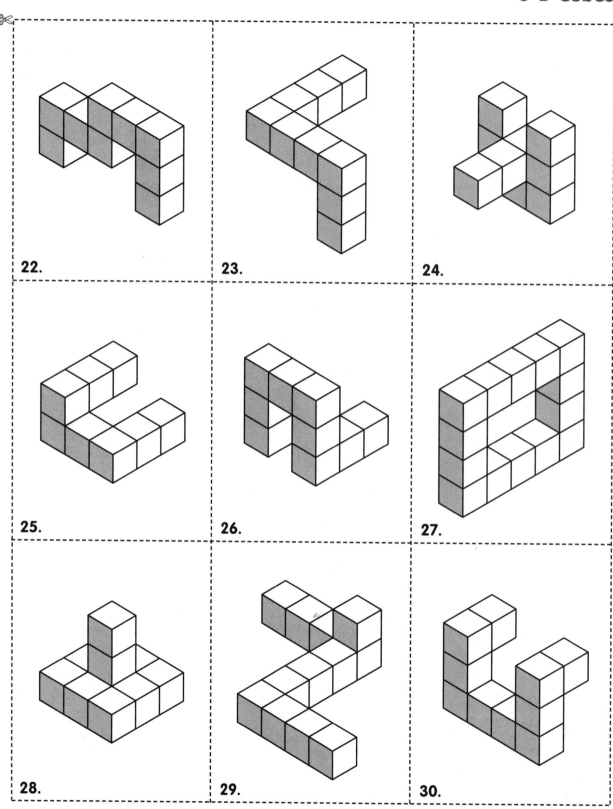

22.

23.

24.

25.

26.

27.

28.

29.

30.

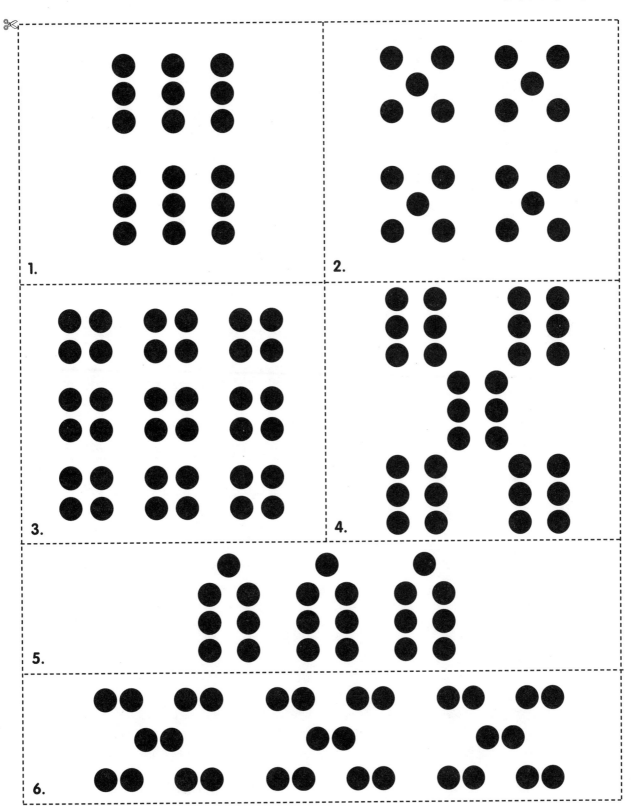

1.

2.

3.

4.

5.

6.

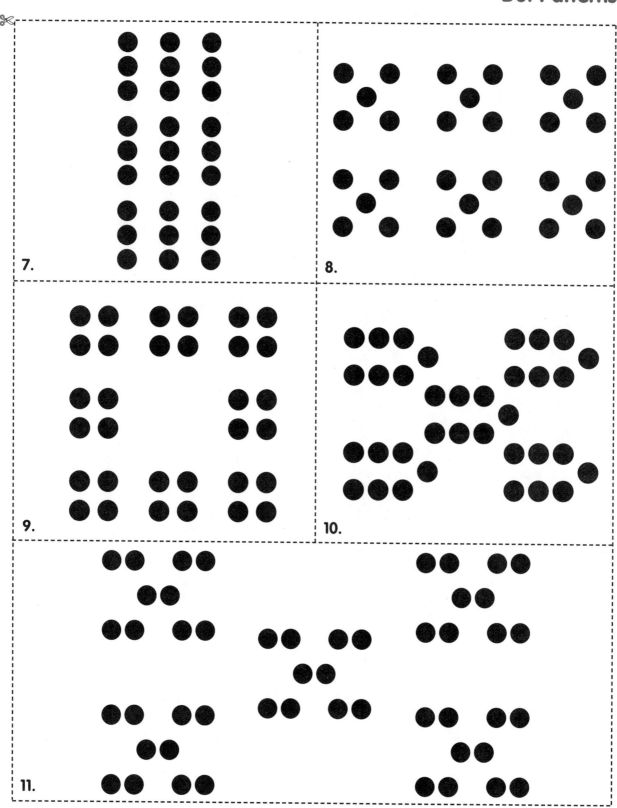

7.

8.

9.

10.

11.

Ten-Minute Math

Length and Perimeter

This is an activity for students who are familiar with the Geo-Logo computer program, although students work off the computer. The task is for students to determine a repeat command to send the Geo-Logo turtle a specified distance. For example, to send the turtle a total distance of 72, they might use this command:

```
repeat 6 [fd 12]
```

In a variation, they determine the repeat command that will form a regular polygon with a specified perimeter.

Mathematical Emphasis

The *Geo-Logo* program helps students make a connection between number and geometry. The "paths" of the turtle become the sides of geometric shapes, and the numbers that students insert in commands such as "repeat" and "forward" (fd) determine the lengths of those sides. In the basic activity, students work only with line segments; in variations, they work with complete polygons. The focus is on

- providing values for variables (the "repeat" number and the "forward" number)
- relating factors to their multiples
- recognizing, visualizing, and drawing polygons
- relating the perimeter of a polygon to the lengths of its sides

Materials
Calculators (optional, for checking work)

Computer and *Geo-Logo* (optional, for testing student plans)

Procedure

Step 1. Specify a distance for the turtle to go. For example, "Using the repeat command, make the turtle go 35 turtle steps."

Step 2. Students write commands to move the turtle that distance. Working in pairs, students spend 2 or 3 minutes writing a list of *Geo-Logo* repeat commands that would send the turtle the specified distance. For example, for 35 turtle steps, these commands would work:

```
repeat 5 [fd 7]

repeat 7 [fd 5]

repeat 35 [fd 1]

repeat 1 [fd 35]
```

Students might use calculators to test their ideas.

Step 3. List all the different responses. Ask students to explain how they know each command works. Students might skip count, demonstrate with concrete materials, or explain their mental strategies to justify their commands. Ask, "Have you found *all* the possibilities for this particular distance? How do you know? Could forward 3 work? What about forward 9? What about forward 14? How do you know?"

Perimeters of Regular Polygons

Present problems that either provide the perimeter of a shape and ask students to find the length of a side, or give the length of a side and ask students to determine the perimeter. For example:

1. The turtle was given this command:

   repeat 4 [fd ? rt 9Ø]

   When it was finished, the turtle had drawn a closed shape with a perimeter of 40 turtle steps. What shape did it make? What is the missing number for the forward command?

2. The turtle made a regular hexagon (a six-sided shape just like the yellow pattern block). The perimeter of the hexagon was 72 turtle steps. This was the command:

   repeat 6 [fd ? rt 6Ø]

   What is the missing number for the forward command?

3. The turtle made a triangle with this command:

   repeat 3 [fd 35 rt 12Ø]

   What is the perimeter of the triangle?

4. The turtle made a regular pentagon with a perimeter of 120 turtle steps. This was the command:

   repeat 5 [fd ? rt 108]

   What is the missing number for the forward command?

For these problems, students sketch what they think the turtle drew and mark on their sketch the lengths of the sides and the perimeter. Optionally, students might act out what the turtle did by walking its path on the floor.

Perimeters of Rectangles

Present problems involving rectangles whose sides are not all equal. For example:

1. The turtle made a rectangle using the following command:

   repeat 2 [fd 2Ø rt 9Ø fd 1Ø rt 9Ø]

   What did the rectangle look like? What is its perimeter?

2. The turtle made a rectangle with a perimeter of 50. It made the shape with this command:

   repeat 2 [fd 12 rt 9Ø fd ? rt 9Ø]

   What is the missing number for the forward command?

3. The turtle made a rectangle with a perimeter of 40. It made the shape with this command:

repeat 2 [fd ? rt 9Ø fd ? rt 9Ø]

What are the missing numbers for the two forward commands? Is there more than one set of numbers that will work?

Students sketch what they think the turtle drew and mark on their sketch the lengths of the sides and the perimeter. As you walk around the room, you can easily see from these sketches what students understand and what is confusing for them as they visualize the turtle's movements. You might also suggest that students act out the turtle's movements.

Using Decimals

Introduce the use of 0.5 into the problems. For example:

The turtle was given the following command:

repeat 4 [fd 6.5]

How many turtle steps did it take?

Special Notes

The Repeat Command in *Geo-Logo*   If your students have not yet used the repeat command on the computer, you will have to introduce it before using this activity. Write a repeat command on the board. Explain that the directions inside the bracket are done over and over again, as many times as the number following the word *repeat*. So, the command repeat 2Ø [fd 2] means: "Take 2 turtle steps (that's the first time), take 2 turtle steps (that's the second time), take 2 turtle steps (that's the third time), and continue taking 2 turtle steps until you've done that 20 times."

Give a few different repeat commands for students to act out. Include some examples with more than one command in the brackets. For example, repeat 4 [fd 1Ø rt 9Ø] means that the turtle will do the two commands fd 1Ø rt 9Ø four times:

fd 10 rt 90 fd 10 rt 90 fd 10 rt 90 fd 10 rt 90

About Perimeter   If students are not familiar with the word *perimeter,* explain that it is the distance around the outside of a closed shape. Draw a closed shape on the board and say: "If an ant started here [*any point*] and walked all the way around the shape until it came back to where it started, it would have walked around the shape's *perimeter.*"

Make some closed shapes on the floor with tape. After students walk around the perimeter of each shape, ask how far they went. They might identify the distance in heel-to-toe footsteps, in paces, or in standard measures. For related activities on linear measure, using both nonstandard and standard units, see the grade 3 *Investigations* unit *From Paces to Feet.*

Testing Students' Commands on the Computer If you have available a computer with a large demonstration screen, you can test students' proposed commands so that everyone can see the results. Otherwise, students can independently test the commands at the computer, using the Free Explore activity in *Geo-Logo*.

There are several ways to test the students' repeat commands to see if the turtle travels the correct distance:

> Have the turtle make the line (for example, forward 35). Then bring the turtle back to the beginning of the line and test each of the student's repeat commands to see if they bring the turtle the same distance.

> Draw a line of the correct length (for example, 35 turtle steps). Position the turtle so that, using the student's repeat command, it will draw a line parallel to the first line. This way students can easily compare the lengths of the two lines.

> Use the Ruler tool in *Geo-Logo* to measure the lines made by students' repeat commands. However, keep in mind that it is easy to be off by one or two turtle steps in measuring with the Ruler. When using the Ruler with decimals, you will want to make sure that numbers are displayed using one decimal point; change the number of decimal places by selecting "Decimal Places" from the Options menu.

Related Homework Option

Turtle Commands at Home   You might assign a group of related problems; for example:

1. Write *Geo-Logo* commands, using *repeat,* to make a line 60 turtle steps long.

2. Draw a few different rectangles that have a perimeter of 60. Label the length and width of each one. Write *Geo-Logo* commands, using *repeat,* that would make each rectangle.

3. Write *Geo-Logo* commands to make regular hexagons. Use this form:

   `repeat 6 [fd ? rt 6Ø]`

   Find the perimeter of each hexagon.

Volume and Surface Area

Looking at a pictured configuration of cubes, which we call a cube building, students figure out its volume (the number of cubes) and its surface area (the number of square "stamps" needed to cover the outside).

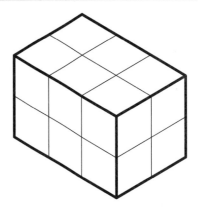

Mathematical Emphasis

Through the Volume and Surface Area activity, students work with the concept that we generally measure the volume of a 3-D solid in terms of the number of unit cubes that fit inside it. We measure the surface of such a solid in terms of the number of unit squares needed to cover it. In order to count these cubes and squares, students must understand the structure of the 3-D object and be able to organize the cubes that fit inside the object and the squares that cover it. Students also compare the surface areas of 3-D objects with the same volume. The focus is on

- understanding the structure of a 3-D object (for example, how its faces fit together)
- organizing and counting cubes that fill simple 3-D solids
- organizing and counting the squares that cover simple 3-D solids
- recognizing that 3-D objects with the same volume do not necessarily have the same surface area

Procedure

Preparation. Cut apart the 20 figures on the Cube Buildings transparencies. Keep the identification number with each figure, because it will help you orient the figure on the overhead. The five figures within Sets A, B, C, and D build on one another and should be presented in sequence, if possible; thus you might clip sets together or store each set in its own envelope.

If students have done this activity before, skip step 1 and start with step 2.

Step 1. Introduce the square "stamp" as a unit of measure. When doing this activity for the first time, show students a cube and sketch the following on the overhead or board.

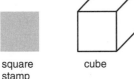

square
stamp

cube

Explain that the stamp is the same size as the square faces of the cube. Ask, "How many square stamps does it take to completely cover a single cube?" Let students examine a cube if they need to.

Materials
Overhead projector

Cube Buildings transparencies (masters provided on pp. 92–93)

Snap™ cubes or other interlocking cubes that connect on all sides, 40–50 for each pair of students

Paper and pencil

Step 2. Display a diagram of a cube building on the overhead. Students work with a partner to figure out how many stamps are needed to cover it and how many cubes are needed to build it. Have cubes available for students to figure or check with. After they have had some experience with this task, encourage them to figure out their answers by looking at the diagrams only, although they can still use cubes to check their answers.

Step 3. Share strategies. Encourage students to look for patterns in the sequence of cube buildings you are presenting and to explain the numerical patterns in terms of spatial organization. For example, the number of stamps needed for building B-3 is just 6 more than the number needed for building B-2, because it has a single additional band or "stripe" of squares (2 on the top, 2 on the bottom, 1 on each side).

B-2 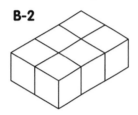   **B-3**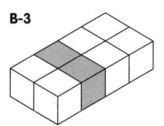

Volume and Surface Area
Variations

Same Volume, Different Surface Area

Changing the Shape   Begin with any 3-D cube building. After students find the volume (number of cubes) and the surface area (number of stamps) for that figure, they rearrange the cubes to make a rectangular solid with the same volume but different dimensions and a different surface area.

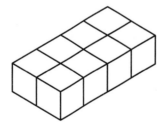 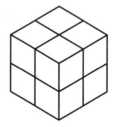

Building with Surface Area in Mind   Students begin with 20 cubes. Using all 20 cubes, they make a building that has a small surface area, then make another building with the 20 cubes that has a larger surface area. Challenge them to discover the largest surface area they could get for a building of 20 cubes.

Working from Outline and Dimensions Only

On the board or overhead, sketch the outline of a cube building that is a rectangular solid, without drawing any of the interior lines that show where the cubes connect. Label the three dimensions of the solid. For example, building D-2 would look like this:

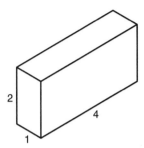

Students work together to find the number of cubes in this building, and the number of square stamps needed to cover it entirely.

Working with Dimensions Only

For an extra challenge, give only the dimensions of a solid, without any visual image. For example, for building D-2, you would give the dimensions 1 by 2 by 4. How many cubes are needed to make it? How many square stamps are needed to cover its surface? Encourage students to solve these problems by drawing their own diagrams instead of using cubes. Give dimensions of larger buildings, such as 3 by 4 by 10.

Volume and Surface Area

Cube Buildings

A-1

B-1

A-2

B-2

A-3

B-3

A-4

B-4

A-5

B-5

Cube Buildings

C-1

D-1

C-2

D-2

C-3

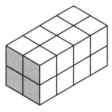

D-3

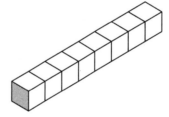

C-4

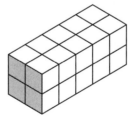

D-4

C-5

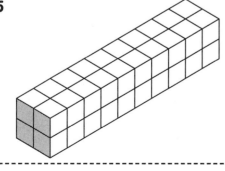

D-5

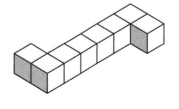

Number Games

The games in this section provide enjoyable practice with number concepts and number relationships. Like the activities for number in the first section of this book, these games offer the chance for repeated computation practice as well as strategic mathematical thinking. Students can play the games independently in small groups, leaving the teacher free to observe or to work with a few students. Once students have learned a game, they can play it many times throughout the year. Games are also a useful link with the home, as parents can learn about their children's mathematical thinking by playing the games with them.

Players use randomly drawn numeral cards to make pairs of numbers that, when added together, make a total as close as possible to 100. They compare answers with one another to determine who has come closest to 100.

Materials

Deck of 44 numeral cards (pp. 100–102) for each group of players

Score sheet (p. 103) for each player, or model setting up a score sheet on regular lined paper

Mathematical Emphasis

While playing Close to 100, students develop strategies for adding two-digit numbers and for comparing two- and three-digit numbers. They have opportunities to estimate sums and differences, to practice addition and subtraction pairs, and to extend their understanding of place value. The focus is on

- exploring combinations of numbers that equal or nearly equal 100
- developing a sense of the relative size of the hundreds, tens, and ones places
- developing strategies for adding and subtracting two- and three-digit numbers

Number of Players

One, two, or three individuals, or teams of two

Procedure

Step 1. Deal the first round. The dealer mixes the deck of numeral cards and deals six cards to each player, or to each pair of players working as a team.

Step 2. Players arrange their cards. Players use any four of their number cards to make two numbers with a total as close as possible to 100. Wild cards can stand for any digit from 0 to 9. A player who is dealt a wild card may declare its value.

Step 3. Players figure and record their scores. They first add the two numbers they have made with the numeral cards. Their score is the difference between that total and 100. Players each write the two numbers they made, the total, and their score on their score sheet.

Step 4. Deal new cards for the next round. Players discard the four cards they used in Round 1, keeping the two they did not use. Then they are dealt four new cards. Each player should always have six cards in each round. Whenever the original deck is used up, the dealer mixes the discard pile and deals again from the top.

Step 5. Repeat for five rounds. Players continue through five rounds and then total their five scores. The lowest total score wins.

Sample game

Round 1

Mark is dealt

Annie is dealt

Mark makes 58 + 29, for a total of 87 and a score of 13.

Annie makes 45 + 57, for a total of 102 and a score of 2.

Round 2

With two cards left from Round 1 and four new ones, Mark holds

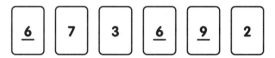

With two cards left from Round 1 and four new ones, Annie holds

Mark makes 36 + 62, for a total of 98 and a score of 2.

Annie makes 98 + 02, for a total of 100 and a score of 0.

Both Mark and Annie could have gotten closer to 100 in Round 1, and Mark could have gotten closer in Round 2. Can you see how?

Close to 100 Score Sheet	Mark		Close to 100 Score Sheet	Annie	
Round 1	58 + 29 = 87	13	Round 1	45 + 57 = 102	2
Round 2	36 + 62 = 98	2	Round 2	98 + 02 = 100	0
Round 3	93 + 06 = 99	1	Round 3	62 + 51 = 113	13
Round 4	50 + 50 = 100	0	Round 4	32 + 67 = 99	1
Round 5	32 + 68 = 100	0	Round 5	75 + 06 = 81	19
	TOTAL	16		TOTAL	35

Using Negative Scores

Players may use negative as well as positive integers in scoring the game. If a player's total is above 100, the score is positive. If the total is below 100, the score is negative. For example, a total of 103 is scored as + 3 (3 more than 100), while a total of 98 is scored as –2. With the variation, the score sheets for the sample game would look like this:

Close to 100 Score Sheet	Mark		Close to 100 Score Sheet	Annie
Round 1 58 + 29 = 87	–13		Round 1 45 + 57 = 102	+2
Round 2 36 + 62 = 98	– 2		Round 2 98 + 02 = 100	0
Round 3 93 + 06 = 99	– 1		Round 3 62 + 51 = 113	+13
Round 4 50 + 50 = 100	0		Round 4 32 + 67 = 99	–1
Round 5 32 + 68 = 100	0		Round 5 75 + 06 = 81	–19
TOTAL	–16		TOTAL	–5

As in the basic game, the player with the total score closest to zero wins. So in this case Annie wins, whereas Mark won the game played without using negative numbers.

Scoring this way changes the strategy for the game. Even though Mark got two perfect scores for making exactly 100 in Rounds 2 and 3, he did not compensate for his negative values with some positive ones. Annie had some totals quite far away from 100, but she balanced her negative and positive scores more evenly to get a total score closer to zero.

Close to 1,000

Materials: Close to 100 Score Sheet (p. 103) or lined paper; numeral cards

For each round, players are dealt eight cards. Players use any six of these to make two numbers that total as close as possible to 1,000. For example, a player who holds 4, 5, 8, 3, 2, 9, 9, and 0 might try 420 + 583 (1,003). The score for each round is the difference between the total and 1,000. As students become comfortable with this version, you might introduce negative and positive integers as a scoring variation. Note that the Close to 100 Score Sheet also works for Close to 1,000, or players can keep track of their scores on lined paper.

Close to 0

Materials: Close to 0 Score Sheet (p. 104) or lined paper; numeral cards

For each round, players are dealt six cards. They use any four cards to make two numbers with a *difference* as close as possible to 0. For example, a player who holds the cards 3, 7, 9, 4, 1, and 6 might make 41 – 39, with a score of 2. Play continues for five rounds, and the lowest total score wins. Players may use the Close to 0 Score Sheet or simply use lined paper to keep track of their two numbers and their scores (the difference between the two numbers) for each round.

Close to 0 with Larger Numbers

Materials: Close to 0 Score Sheet or lined paper; numeral cards

For three-digit numbers, players are given eight cards. They use any six cards to make two three-digit numbers with a difference is as close as possible to 0.

0	0	0	0
1	1	1	1
2	2	2	2
3	3	3	3

4	4	4	4
5	5	5	5
<u>6</u>	<u>6</u>	<u>6</u>	<u>6</u>
7	7	7	7

8	8	8	8
9	9	9	9
Wild Card	Wild Card	Wild Card	Wild Card

Close to 100

You can use this sheet for either Close to 100 or Close to 1,000. There is room to record two games.

Name: _____   Score

Round 1 _____ + _____ = _____   _____

Round 2 _____ + _____ = _____   _____

Round 3 _____ + _____ = _____   _____

Round 4 _____ + _____ = _____   _____

Round 5 _____ + _____ = _____   _____

                                            TOTAL SCORE   _____

Name: _____   Score

Round 1 _____ + _____ = _____   _____

Round 2 _____ + _____ = _____   _____

Round 3 _____ + _____ = _____   _____

Round 4 _____ + _____ = _____   _____

Round 5 _____ + _____ = _____   _____

                                            TOTAL SCORE   _____

Close to 100

Use this sheet for the Close to 0 variation. There is room to record two games.

Name: _____   Score

Round 1 _____ – _____ = _____   _____

Round 2 _____ – _____ = _____   _____

Round 3 _____ – _____ = _____   _____

Round 4 _____ – _____ = _____   _____

Round 5 _____ – _____ = _____   _____

TOTAL SCORE   _____

_____

Name: _____   Score

Round 1 _____ – _____ = _____   _____

Round 2 _____ – _____ = _____   _____

Round 3 _____ – _____ = _____   _____

Round 4 _____ – _____ = _____   _____

Round 5 _____ – _____ = _____   _____

TOTAL SCORE   _____

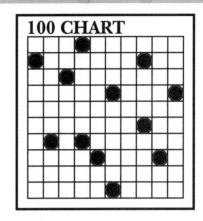

100 CHART

This game uses the 100 chart as a gameboard with 12 translucent markers placed randomly on the numbered squares. Players move around the gameboard trying to capture markers by landing on those squares. They determine a move by putting together combinations of Change cards (with the numbers +1, –1, +2, –2, +3, –3, +10, –10, +20, –20, +30, and –30). The first player or team to capture five markers wins the game.

Mathematical Emphasis

Capture 5 involves students in thinking about addition and subtraction of multiples of 1 and 10. The focus is on

- operating with ones and tens on the 100 chart
- doing calculations with addition and subtraction
- using equations to record a series of changes to a starting number

Number of Players

Two (or two teams)

Procedure

Step 1. Set up the gameboard. Together, players place 12 markers randomly on the 100 chart, so that each marker is on a different number. Each player (or team) then puts a game piece on any uncovered number.

Step 2. Deal the Change cards. The dealer deals out five Change cards, face up, to each player or team. The remaining cards are placed face down.

Step 3. Players take turns trying to capture a marker on the board. Players decide together how to determine who starts. On each turn, a player tries to land on a number with a marker, by moving his or her game piece the amount shown on any Change card or any combination of Change cards. A player who lands on a number with a marker captures the marker by taking it off the board, leaving the game piece in its place. A player can capture only one marker during a turn and cannot move beyond that square in the same turn. Players ending up on a square without a marker must leave their game piece there until their next turn.

Step 4. Players record their moves as equations. To record their moves after each turn, players write an equation on lined paper. For example, a player who begins on 45 and uses the cards +2, –10, +3 would write $45 + 2 - 10 + 3 = 40$.

Materials

100 chart (p. 107) for each group of players

Deck of 40 Change cards (pp. 108–109) for each group of players

Markers (translucent counting chips work best), 12 for each group

Game piece (such as a small colored cube), one for each player or each team

Lined paper for recording "moves"

Step 5. Continue play until there is a winner. After each turn, players place the used Change cards face up in a discard pile and draw cards from the top of the deck to replace the used cards. They always start each turn with five Change cards. As the deck is used up, mix up the discard pile and turn it face down to create a new deck. The first player to capture five markers wins.

Capture 5 Variations

Capture Less

For a shorter version of the game, play Capture 3, in which capturing three markers wins.

Capture More

For a longer game, play continues until all markers have been captured. The player with more markers wins.

Capture All

Play this version cooperatively or as a solitaire game. The object is to capture all 12 markers in as few turns as possible. Players may use either one or two game pieces. If using two game pieces, they may move a single piece during a turn or split the moves between the two pieces. Each piece that ends up on a marker captures it, so with two game pieces, it is possible to capture two markers on a turn.

100 Chart

1	2	3	4	5	6	7	8	9	10
11	12	13	14	15	16	17	18	19	20
21	22	23	24	25	26	27	28	29	30
31	32	33	34	35	36	37	38	39	40
41	42	43	44	45	46	47	48	49	50
51	52	53	54	55	56	57	58	59	60
61	62	63	64	65	66	67	68	69	70
71	72	73	74	75	76	77	78	79	80
81	82	83	84	85	86	87	88	89	90
91	92	93	94	95	96	97	98	99	100

Change Cards (Ones)

+1	+1	+1	+1
–1	–1	–1	–1
+2	+2	+2	+2
–2	–2	–2	–2
+3	+3	–3	–3

+10	+10	+10	+10
−10	−10	−10	−10
+20	+20	+20	+20
−20	−20	−20	−20
+30	+30	−30	−30

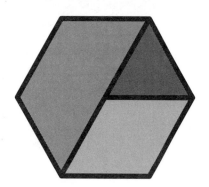

Players try to be the first to make a given number of whole "cookies" (hexagonal pattern blocks) by fitting together pieces on their Hexagon Cookie Sheet. They roll a fraction die or draw fraction cards to determine what fraction they may add each time.

Materials

From one to three fraction dice in two colors for each playing group. Each die should have the fractions $1/2$, $1/2$, $1/3$, $2/3$, $1/6$, and $5/6$. If dice are not available, use sets of fraction cards, six cards per set (p. 112)

Set of pattern blocks for each playing group; remove small tan rhombi and orange squares, leaving only yellow hexagons, red trapezoids, blue rhombi, and green triangles

Hexagon Cookie Sheet (p. 113) for each player

Colored pencils, markers, or crayons

Mathematical Emphasis

By playing the Fraction Cookie Game, students get practice in recognizing and visualizing common fraction combinations based on sixths, such as $1/3 + 1/6 = 1/2$. The focus is on

- identifying fractional parts
- exchanging equivalent fractions
- adding and subtracting fractions
- relating numerical fractions to equivalent visual representations

Number of Players

Two or three

Procedure

Step 1. Set up the game materials. Each group needs a set of pattern blocks (yellow, red, blue, and green only), one fraction die or a set of six fraction cards, and one Hexagon Cookie Sheet for each player. Players put the pattern blocks in a pile between them. Before beginning, players decide together how many cookies someone must make with the pattern blocks in order to win the game. For the basic game, 3–6 cookies is usually enough.

Step 2. Players take turns collecting fractional amounts of cookies. Each player in turn rolls the die or draws a card, picks a pattern block that matches the fractional amount shown, and adds the block to the Hexagon Cookie Sheet. A player may break any fraction into smaller parts. For example, if the fraction is $1/3$, the player may either take a blue diamond ($1/3$ of a hexagon cookie) or two green triangles (each $1/6$ of a hexagon cookie). With the second option, the player can place one triangle to complete a cookie and the other to start a new cookie.

Step 3. At the end of a turn, the player "trades up" as far as possible. In trading up, players must exchange combinations of two or more smaller pattern blocks within a cookie for single larger pieces that are equal to those combinations. Thus, players should have on their sheets the fewest possible pattern blocks at the end of each turn. For example, a player with $2\frac{1}{2}$ cookies should have 1 red (for the $\frac{1}{2}$) and 2 yellow pattern blocks. (If yellow hexagons are in short supply, players might color the sheet to record their completed cookies.) After each round, players check one another's work. When using fraction cards, the player replaces the card drawn and the set is mixed again before the next turn.

Step 4. Continue play until there is a winner. The first player to completely fill in the established target number of hexagon cookies wins.

Adding Fractions

To increase the level of difficulty, add another fraction die to the game. Players now throw two dice (or draw two cards) and add the fractions to determine how much cookie to take. As in the basic game, players finish their turn by "trading up" to end with the fewest possible pieces, and by checking one another's work. The goal is to collect the target number of whole cookies.

Subtracting Fractions

Each player begins with 3–6 whole cookies on the Hexagon Cookie Sheet. Players take turns rolling either one or two dice or drawing fraction cards, and subtract the resulting fractional amount from their cookies. The goal is to be the first player with no cookies left. Players must finish with the exact fraction; for example, a player with $\frac{1}{6}$ of a cookie left cannot remove it with $\frac{1}{2}$; the fraction on the die or card must show $\frac{1}{6}$. Players might play with only one die or with two dice throughout the game; or, the number of dice used could be a choice the player makes for each turn, depending on the fraction needed.

Adding and Subtracting

For a more advanced game, introduce a third die of a different color. Players now roll two dice of one color and a third die of a different color, adding the amounts on the first two and subtracting the amount on the third. The result is added to their cookie collection. (Players may start the game with two hexagon cookies so they won't run out in case the amount to be subtracted is larger than the amount added.) Again, players "trade up" and check one another's work at the end of each turn.

This variation can also be played with fraction cards; simply provide an additional set copied on paper of a different color or marked with colored markers. Players draw two cards of the same color and one card of the other color, and follow the same procedure as with dice.

One set contains six cards, corresponding to a six-sided fraction die. There are two sets on this sheet.

Use these if you don't have fraction dice. Each group of players will need from one to three sets of cards, depending on the version of the game being played. For the variation Adding and Subtracting, they need two sets in one color and a third set in a different color.

$\frac{1}{6}$	$\frac{5}{6}$	$\frac{1}{2}$
$\frac{2}{3}$	$\frac{1}{3}$	$\frac{1}{2}$

$\frac{1}{6}$	$\frac{5}{6}$	$\frac{1}{2}$
$\frac{2}{3}$	$\frac{1}{3}$	$\frac{1}{2}$

Hexagon Cookie Sheet

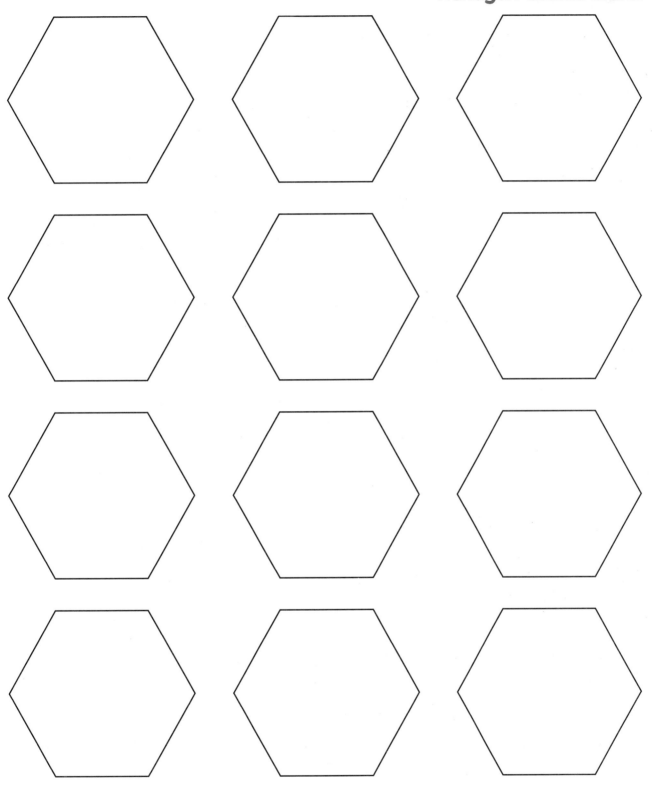

Players choose a target number such as 1,000 and rearrange randomly drawn digits to make numbers as close as possible to that target. For a whole-group game, the teacher selects the digits and players work individually to build a number. They compare solutions in a whole-class discussion or in small groups. For a small-group game, players have their own deck of digit cards and take turns drawing digits for everyone in the group to work with.

Materials

Set of 12 digit cards for each group of players (p. 117)

Paper and pencil

Mathematical Emphasis

Through the Digits Game, students build their understanding of place value, relationships among the places, and the role of zero in a place value system. As they determine how far from the target their numbers are, they develop strategies for comparing. Some students use mental addition or subtraction, others use written addition and subtraction, and others rely on numerical reasoning. The focus is on

- reasoning about place value
- determining which of a set of numbers is closest to a target number
- developing strategies for comparing numbers

Number of Players

Whole class or small groups

Procedure

Step 1. Pick a target number. Choose a number to use as a target number, for example, 1,000.

Step 2. Randomly select the digits to be used. Mix the digit cards face down and draw one for each place in the target number, plus one more. For 1,000, a group would draw five cards.

Step 3. Players arrange the digits. Using paper and pencil, players arrange any number of the selected digits, trying to make a number that is as close as possible to the target number. If the digits picked were 9, 2, 4, 1, and 0, then 1,024 would be the closest anyone could get to the target number of 1,000.

Step 4. Share solutions. Players compare their solutions to see who has come closest to the target number.

Large Targets

To increase the level of difficulty, increase the size of the target number. For example, with the target of 1,000,000, players draw eight digit cards and try to make a number as close to a million as they can.

Largest or Smallest Number

Players draw a specified number of digit cards, and their goal is to make either the largest or the smallest number possible using all those digits.

Largest or Smallest Sum

Players draw a specified number of digit cards and create a two-part addition problem with them, making either the largest or the smallest sum possible. Decide on rules for the combinations of numbers. For example, with four digits drawn, players might be expected to make a two-digit plus a two-digit addition problem, or perhaps a three-digit plus a one-digit problem.

For example, if the digits drawn were 4, 3, 2, and 1, and the rule was using two-digit numbers, then the largest sum possible would be 73 (41 + 32 or 42 + 31), and the smallest sum would be 37 (14 + 23 or 13 + 24). If the rules allowed adding a three-digit and a one-digit number, then 432 + 1 would give the largest sum, and 123 + 4 the smallest.

Largest or Smallest Difference

Following the procedures for Largest or Smallest Sum, players make subtraction problems with the largest and smallest differences.

Largest or Smallest Product

Following the procedures for Largest or Smallest Sum, players make multiplication problems with the largest and smallest products.

Largest or Smallest Decimal

For this and all decimal variations, use a decimal point card in addition to digits selected from the deck. Note that the decimal point card is not mixed with the rest of the digits, but is held out for use on each turn. Players create the largest or smallest decimal numbers they can with a given set of digits. They must place the decimal point to the *left* of their first digit.

Target Decimals

Players create a decimal number that is as close as possible to a target number, which may be either smaller or larger than 1. In this variation, they may choose where to put the decimal point.

Decimal Sums, Differences, Products

Players create addition, subtraction, or multiplication problems using decimal numbers. You may establish restrictions, as described for the Largest or Smallest Sum variation. Players may use two decimal point cards.

One by One

For this variation, each player needs a set of 12 digit cards. Set any goal suggested in other variations (make the largest number, the smallest number, the number closest to a target, and so forth) and tell players how many cards to draw in all. They then begin to draw cards one by one. As each card is turned over and before the next is flipped, the player must decide in which position to place that digit for the best chance of reaching the goal. Once a digit is placed, it cannot be moved during that round.

1	2	3	4
5	<u>6</u>	7	8
<u>9</u>	0	0	0

● ● Decimal point cards for
decimal variations

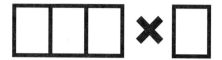

The game leader presents a template for a computation problem (such as _ _ _ × _ _), deals a number card to fill each slot, and then reveals the problem. Players must quickly estimate the answer. At the end of each round, players determine their scores by finding the difference between their estimate and the actual answer.

Materials

Deck of 20 digit cards (p. 121) for each group of players

Calculator (one, for the leader)

Timer that shows seconds

Paper and pencil for recording scores

Mathematical Emphasis

The Estimation Game offers practice with attending to the value of numbers in a problem and anticipating the effect of the operation. The focus is on

- approximating numbers in a problem with round numbers
- doing mental estimation
- finding the difference between an estimate and the exact answer

Number of Players

Four or more

Procedure

Step 1. Choose a problem template. Players take turns being the leader. The leader chooses a problem template like the examples shown. It may involve addition, subtraction, multiplication, or division. A template may use single-digit or multidigit numbers or a combination of these, and may include decimals or fractions.

Examples:

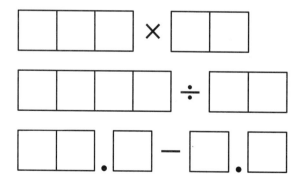

Step 2. Place digits to establish the problem without disclosing it. The leader draws one card for each slot in the template and records the digits, in the order drawn, without showing anyone. For example:

Template: ☐☐☐ × ☐☐

Cards dealt: 7 4 1 0 3

Recorded problem: **741 × 03**

Because of the random way numeral cards are drawn, 0 will sometimes turn up as the leftmost digit of a number. Players need to understand that 090 is the same as 90, and 03 is the same as 3. However, if they end up with a problem that requires dividing by 0 (such as 491 ÷ 0), the leader should draw a new card to replace the 0.

Step 3. Reveal the problem for timed estimates. The leader discloses the problem to the group and starts timing. Players have exactly 30 seconds to estimate the answer mentally, without pencil or paper. Players write down their estimated answer, but not their computation steps.

Step 4. Find the actual answer and compare with players' estimates. After time is up, the leader finds the actual answer with the calculator. Players record their own estimate and the actual answer on lined paper, writing the larger number first. The difference between the two numbers is their score. If the answer is a decimal number, players may agree to approximate the exact answer to a whole number before finding the difference.

Step 5. Repeat with the same template and different digits. Using the same problem template, the leader deals new numeral cards for rounds 2 and 3.

Quick Thinking

Increase the level of difficulty by asking that players make their estimates within 15 seconds.

Larger or Smaller Numbers

Adjust the difficulty level of the problem for particular groups by providing templates with more digits or fewer digits.

Estimate and Compute

For computation practice, players can finish each round by finding the actual answer without using a calculator. Players should agree on the actual answer before recording it and finding their score.

Beat the Teacher

Do one problem each day with a student leader. The teacher is one of the players. The goal is to beat the teacher, who also must estimate the answer within 30 seconds.

0	0	1	1
2	2	3	3
4	4	5	5
<u>6</u>	<u>6</u>	7	7
8	8	<u>9</u>	<u>9</u>

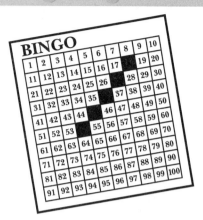

In these two versions of the classic game, the "Bingo" grid is either the 100 chart (for Multiple Bingo) or the multiplication table through 12 (for Division Bingo). Players select number cards from special decks and find either a multiple or a factor of that number on their Bingo grid, then color in that square. The goal is to color in five consecutive numbers, horizontally, vertically, or diagonally.

Materials

Grid for Multiple Bingo (p. 125)

Multiple Bingo number pool (p. 126), set of 20 cards for each playing group

Grid for Division Bingo (p. 127) for each player

Division Bingo number pool (p. 128), set of 20 cards for each playing group

Crayon or marker for each player

Calculators for players to share

Mathematical Emphasis

These Bingo games offer practice with finding multiples and factors of numbers. Whether players skip count, use multiplication pairs, or divide to find suitable numbers on their grid, they are reasoning numerically about the relationships among factors and their multiples. The focus is on

- relating factors to their multiples
- becoming familiar with multiplication patterns
- developing number sense about multiplication and division relationships

Number of Players

Groups of two to four

Procedure

Step 1: Gather the materials. Each player needs a "Bingo" grid (the 100 chart for playing Multiple Bingo, or the multiplication table for playing Division Bingo) and a crayon or marker. The cards for the number pool (16 number cards and 4 wild cards) are stacked face down.

Step 2: The caller turns up the top card in the number pool. Players take turns being the caller. Any time the caller turns up a wild card, he or she can name any number as the factor or the number to be divided.

Step 3: Players decide individually which number to color on their Bingo grid. For Multiple Bingo, players may color in any number that is a multiple of the number (factor) called. They also write the factor in the square. For example, if the caller turns up a 5, players could color any one of the numbers 5, 10, 15, 20, 25, and so forth. In the corner of the square selected, the player writes the factor 5.

For Division Bingo, the procedure is the same, except that players use the multiplication table for a Bingo grid and color in a *factor* of the number that is turned up. As before, the player writes the number called in the selected square. For example, if the caller turns up 100, players could color in any one of the numbers 1, 2, 4, 5, 10, 20, 25, 50, or 100, and write 100 in the corner of the chosen square.

Step 4: Repeat the process until someone has colored five in a row. The game continues until a player colors in five numbers in a row. The remaining players can choose to continue until they also get five in a row.

Special Notes

Game Strategies   A player who gets to name a wild card number should strategically choose a number that helps his or her own game without helping the other players. For example, in Multiple Bingo, it is often useful to pick a prime number. Thus, while the player might pick 23 to fill in a gap between other multiples already colored on his or her grid, other players would be limited to the choice of 23, 46, 69, or 92.

Whole-Class Game   While the procedure describes a small-group game, either version of Bingo could played as a whole class. One caller is named to turn up the numbers for the group. If a wild card is turned up, the caller names a number for everyone to use. You might continue play until you have one winner or until every player has covered five in a row. When playing as a whole group, students who are new to the game might collaborate with another student.

Using Materials for Reference   Encourage students to use calculators as a reference tool for checking multiples and factors.

Reusing the Bingo Grids   To reuse the Bingo grids from one game to the next, students might use chips or small cubes to cover the squares instead of coloring them. Alternatively, some teachers prepare laminated grids that can be wiped off after each game, with players using either a crayon or an overhead marker.

Limiting the Number Pool

For an easier version of Multiple Bingo, use only the top two rows of number cards plus a few wild cards. This means that students will be finding multiples for only 2, 3, 4, and 5. If your students have 100 charts from their class work that highlight these multiples, they might use those charts for reference while they play the game. As students become familiar with additional multiples, add cards to the number pool accordingly. Similarly, an easier version of Division Bingo would use only 100, 180, 200, 60, 98, 32, 72, and 150, plus wild cards, in the number pool.

Multiple Bingo and Division Bingo Variations

Limiting the 100 Chart

When students first play Multiple Bingo, they will tend to color in only "easy" numbers—especially single-digit numbers and multiples of 10. Here are some ways to encourage them to use more difficult numbers:

Block out the top row and right-hand column of the 100 chart; these numbers may not be used in the game.

Establish a rule that players must start with a number near the middle of the grid.

Give bonus points for a win on a diagonal (with only corners of squares touching). This may encourage players to notice the nines and elevens tables on the two main diagonals.

Related Homework Option

Students can play either version of Bingo at home with the appropriate materials.

Multiple Bingo

1	2	3	4	5	6	7	8	9	10
11	12	13	14	15	16	17	18	19	20
21	22	23	24	25	26	27	28	29	30
31	32	33	34	35	36	37	38	39	40
41	42	43	44	45	46	47	48	49	50
51	52	53	54	55	56	57	58	59	60
61	62	63	64	65	66	67	68	69	70
71	72	73	74	75	76	77	78	79	80
81	82	83	84	85	86	87	88	89	90
91	92	93	94	95	96	97	98	99	100

2	**2**	**2**	**3**
3	**4**	**4**	**5**
<u>6</u>	**7**	**8**	**<u>9</u>**
12	**15**	**16**	**20**
Wild Card	**Wild Card**	**Wild Card**	**Wild Card**

Division Bingo

	1	2	3	4	5	6	7	8	9	10	11	12
1	1	2	3	4	5	6	7	8	9	10	11	12
2	2	4	6	8	10	12	14	16	18	20	22	24
3	3	6	9	12	15	18	21	24	27	30	33	36
4	4	8	12	16	20	24	28	32	36	40	44	48
5	5	10	15	20	25	30	35	40	45	50	55	60
6	6	12	18	24	30	36	42	48	54	60	66	72
7	7	14	21	28	35	42	49	56	63	70	77	84
8	8	16	24	32	40	48	56	64	72	80	88	96
9	9	18	27	36	45	54	63	72	81	90	99	108
10	10	20	30	40	50	60	70	80	90	100	110	120
11	11	22	33	44	55	66	77	88	99	110	121	132
12	12	24	36	48	60	72	84	96	108	120	132	144

Number Pool for Division Bingo

100	180	200	60
98	32	72	150
240	144	324	225
448	396	330	450
Wild Card	Wild Card	Wild Card	Wild Card

Ten-Minute Math in Investigations

Ten-Minute
Math

For teachers who are coordinating this *Ten-Minute Math* book with their use of the *Investigations in Number, Data, and Space* curriculum, the chart on the facing page indicates the units in which the activities appear, usually as part of the Ten-Minute Math feature of the program. When the activity or game is used in classwork as part of an investigation rather than as Ten-Minute Math, the unit names in the chart are shown in italics. Following are some other explanatory notes on individual activities:

- Some teachers will recognize Calendar Math as an extension of Today's Date, a classroom routine appearing in the grade 2 units.
- The game Capture 5 did not originally appear in any units for grades 3–5. Designed for grade 2 and introduced in the unit *Putting Together and Taking Apart,* Capture 5 has since proved valuable for students in grades 3–5 as well.
- Division Bingo is the same game that is sometimes called Factor Bingo in the *Investigations* curriculum.

	Grade 3 Units	Grade 4 Units	Grade 5 Units
NUMBER			
Calender Math	Mathematical Thinking at Grade 3 Landmarks in the Hundreds		
Counting Around the Class	Things That Come in Groups Landmarks in the Hundreds	Arrays and Shares Landmarks in the Thousands	Containers and Cubes
Seeing Numbers			Name That Portion
Guess My Number (and Guess My Unit)	Fair Shares	Different Shapes, Equal Pieces Packages and Groups	Measurement Benchmarks Containers and Cubes
Estimation and Number Sense	From Paces to Feet Up and Down the Number Line Combining and Comparing	Mathematical Thinking at Grade 4 The Shape of the Data	Measurement Benchmarks
Broken Calculator	Flips, Turns, and Area Fair Shares	The Shape of the Data Changes Over Time	
Nearest Answer			Between Never and Always Patterns of Change
DATA AND PROBABILITY			
Likely or Unlikely?	Things That Come in Groups	Money, Miles, and Large Numbers	
Exploring Data	Mathematical Thinking at Grade 3 Combining and Comparing	Mathematical Thinking at Grade 4 Packages and Groups	Mathematical Thinking at Grade 5 Name That Portion
What Is Likely?	Exploring Solids and Boxes	Landmarks in the Thousands Three Out of Four Like Spaghetti	Building on Numbers You Know
Guess My Rule	*Mathematical Thinking at Grade 3*	*Three Out of Four Like Spaghetti*	*Picturing Polygons*
Graph Stories		*Changes Over Time*	Patterns of Change
GEOMETRY AND SHAPE			
Quick Images	From Paces to Feet Exploring Solids and Boxes	Changes Over Time Seeing Solids and Silhouettes	Mathematical Thinking at Grade 5 Building on Numbers You Know
Length and Perimeter	Turtle Paths	Sunken Ships and Grid Patterns	
Volume and Surface Area			Data: Kids, Cats and Ads
NUMBER GAMES			
Close to 100 (and Close to 1000)	*Combining and Comparing*	*Mathematical Thinking at Grade 4* *Landmarks in the Thousands* *Money, Miles, and Large Numbers*	*Mathematical Thinking at Grade 5*
Capture 5			
Fraction Cookie Game	*Fair Shares*		
Digits Game			Data: Kids, Cats, and Ads
Estimation Game			Building on Numbers You Know
Multiple Bingo and Division Bingo		*Arrays and Shares* *Packages and Groups*	Picturing Polygons